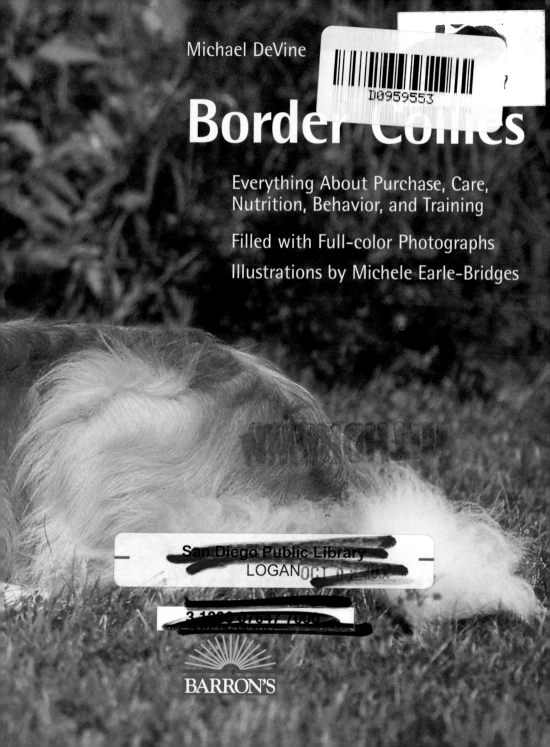

Michael DeVine

D0959553

Border Collies

Everything About Purchase, Care, Nutrition, Behavior, and Training

Filled with Full-color Photographs

Illustrations by Michele Earle-Bridges

BARRON'S

2 CONTENTS

A BRIEF HISTORY OF THE BORDER COLLIE

Border Collies have always been practical dogs—workers and companions to their owners. Recently that has all changed. Border Collies are more often seen in suburbs and cities than farms. Treated well they have a sweet disposition and get along well with children and pets.

Origin

Border Collies are a relatively new breed; shepherds have been using "collies" for centuries. The term "collie" originally meant "black" in some border and Scottish dialects. Over time the term became synonymous with the shepherds' dogs, regardless of their color. Early writings describe the dogs only as being medium-sized, quick, and slender. Photographs taken in the earliest days of photography show working stockdogs all over Britain. These dogs varied greatly in appearance. One picture of a working female, taken around 1850, shows an animal with the size and general body structure of the modern Border Collie. This particular female, however, had the wiry hair most commonly associated with Airedales.

Although Border Collies have become popular as pets, as well as flyball and obedience competitors, their history lies in working sheep and cattle.

Sheepdogs

Sheep have always been an important part of the economy in rural Britain and sheepdogs were the core of the economy. Without them, controlling sheep in the open moors and mountains would be an "iffy" proposition. Sheepmen of the country needed a dog that would move sheep as quietly and gently as possible. They also needed an animal that would do most of the footwork for them.

Prior to 1873 there were a variety of working cattle- and sheepdogs in Great Britain. The dogs showed all types of hair coat, ranged widely in size, and differed greatly in color. Some animals had "white" eyes while most had eyes in one of the shades of brown.

Fetching Dogs

Most of the recent ancestors of the Border Collie were fetching dogs. Fetching dogs have an instinctive tendency to go around stock and bring them back toward the handler. According

This Border Collie is moving a small group of sheep as its instinct, and a little training, tells it to.

to Matt Mundell, a chronicler of British rural life and a lover of Border Collies, most of the dogs of the late 1800s were a noisy lot. At the large sheep gathers of the time, the normal noise of the sheep was augmented by the whistles and shouts of shepherds and the constant barking of their sheepdogs. Dogs of the day were prone to nip and bite and to move about in the manner of Australian Shepherds and Australian Cattle Dogs. Working style varied from dog to dog as much as physical appearance.

Modern Border Collies

Modern Border Collies are typified by a working style that involves a quiet, head-down style that is remarkably similar to a wolf creeping up on its prey. Instead of barking and nipping excessively, Border Collies use "eye." A Border Collie with strong "eye" will stare at bunched stock until they decide there are better places to be. Some people are even a little put off by the breed's tendency to stare at them.

Trials

It was in 1873 that the first sheepdog trial was held in Bala, Wales. Prior to this first trial, every good sheepdog in Britain had local support and little other notoriety. Before 1873 the working sheepdog situation was entirely provincial. Every village had a best dog and it was touted to every other village as being the best in the world.

The trial of 1873 put sheepdog work on an empirical basis. Every dog ran the same course; every dog got sheep that were roughly the same. Suddenly, the top dog from village X and the top dog from village Y could be com-

This Border Collie might not fit your expectations, but it is fully a Border Collie.

pared in some meaningful way. Good dogs and good handlers had to either "put up or shut up." The better dogs were selected for breeding on the basis of their success in trials. It was Britain's system of trials that eventually created the modern Border Collie.

Twenty years after the first trial, a dog named Hemp was born in the kennels of a well-known trainer and handler, Adam Telfer. Hemp was a calm working dog that moved sheep quietly and efficiently in contrast to other, noisier breeds. His style of work was so impressive that within a few generations there were few working collies in Britain without his genes and some semblance of his working style. Hemp is considered the foundation sire of all Border Collies. Although there have been a number of notable dogs called Hemp, "Old Hemp" refers to Adam Telfer's great dog from the turn of the century.

The Standard

Hemp provided both the genes and the working style common to modern Border Collies, but the breed had no standard. When the International Sheepdog Trials Society was formed in 1906, one of the first things it did was to establish rules for competition. These rules were put into action that same year. It is this set of rules that served as *the* standard for Border Collies ever since. It is a working standard. The dog meeting the standard had to be able do something well—work sheep. It mattered not one bit what the dog looked like as long as it was good at its job. These rules have created the modern Border Collie.

British shepherds and farmers have always just referred to dogs used to move sheep as "sheepdogs." To this day, Border Collies, Bearded Collies, and other breeds are just "sheepdogs" to the working sheepman. It was not until 1915 that James Reid, the secretary of the International Sheepdog Society (ISDS) referred to the breed as "Border Collies." It is likely that name was used casually before Mr. Reid used it. His was the first official use of the name that anyone can find. This, of course, referred to the breed's origins in the border areas of England and Scotland. Mr. Reid apparently felt that the term "sheepdog" was not specific enough for the dog that his organization was developing

The herding instinct is so strong that young dogs will try to herd blowing leaves, drifting snow, or each other.

and by this time the term "Collie" was being used almost exclusively for Standard Collies.

Famous Border Collies

Herdsman's Tommy, a descendant of Hemp, was another important Border Collie sire. Tommy was described as an unattractive, strong-willed dog that could not be managed on the trial course. He never won the International but two of his sons won the 1907 and 1913 Supreme Championships. According to Eric Halsall, 27 of the 29 dogs that won Supreme Championships between 1906 and 1951 were direct descendants of Tommy's. Every one of the 20 Supreme Champions from 1960 to 1979 were from Tommy's bloodlines. Even Wiston Cap, recognized as the greatest trial dog of all time, boasted Herdsman's Tommy as an ancestor. Tommy is not on the list of National and Supreme champions but he has done his bit for the breed by providing strength and self-confidence to his descendants.

A dog by the name of Kep, owned by James Scott, won the International trials in 1908 and 1909. Kep was a master both on the trial course and in the fields. He was described as being a quiet, well-balanced, intelligent dog. He was only distantly connected to Adam Telfer's Hemp lines although his working style was very similar. This lack of genetic overlap was Kep's contribution to the breed. His existence has been credited with saving the Border Collie breed by reducing the inbreeding that had begun due to Old Hemp's popularity as a stud.

Jim Wilson's Roy took a little different tack on things than some of the Border Collies that went before him. Roy started with a number of handicaps. He had been stunted by a bout of distemper as a puppy. Later, he lost most of the vision in one eye as the result of a fight with his half-brother. In spite of these problems, Roy went on to win six International and five National Championships. Included in his Championship count were the 1934, 1936, and 1937 Supreme Championships. Roy's blood flows in the veins of a large percentage of modern Border Collies.

A Border Collie that has been highly influential in recent years is Whitehope Nap. Nap's best finish in the Internationals was a reserve in 1955. Even though he never took the Supreme Championship, handlers and trainers all over Britain swear by his descendants. Nap puppies are so quick-witted and sure of themselves that only quick-thinking handlers are able to deal with them. Nap's bloodlines produced a majority of the International winners during the 1960s and 1970s. If you look closely at the more successful Border Collies in Obedience you will see the self-confidence and independence provided by Nap.

A working Border Collie waits to move some cows.

The 1965 International Champion, Wiston Cap, was marked for greatness as a puppy. At the age of six months he was already working on the farm, even though it is not normal practice. He won his first trial at ten months of age. At the age of 23 months he won the International Championship. Wiston Cap's performance on the British trial scene was phenomenal. Farmers, shepherds, and smallholders from all over Britain bred their prized females to him in just the same way that they had bred to Hemp in his heyday. Not only was he a great worker, Cap has since proven his greatness as a stud. Three of his sons and two of his grandsons have won the Supreme Championship, a record that underscores the quality of Cap and his ancestors.

In 1923 Sam Stoddard of Bradford, Connecticut, imported that year's International Champion, George Brown's Spot. Sam, an expatriate Scottish shepherd, knew the value of the working Border Collie. Working with Spot, Sam soon let the people of the United States know how valuable Border Collies could be to the sheepman. They became important to the breed due to the number of exhibitions they put on at fairs and agricultural gatherings. In later years, Stoddard and Spot would win numerous trials. He was also instrumental in the formation of the North American Sheepdog Society. Sam Stoddard was voted first president and Spot was registered as the Number One dog in the NASDS's books.

There are more Border Collies that have proved important to the breed than can be named here. Certainly, Wilson's Cap, Bosworth Coon, and John Gilchrist's Spot should be mentioned as important to the history of the breed. All these dogs have won the highest prize that a Border Collie can win, the International Supreme Championship. It is important to note that these dogs ranged greatly in size, color, and hair coat. The only things they had to identify themselves as a breed were extreme intelligence, instinctive stock sense, and a quiet working style.

ARE YOU BORDER COLLIE MATERIAL?

Although Border Collies are wonderful dogs, they are not for everyone. They are active and curious dogs, more so than most. If owners are not appropriate to the breed, problems can arise for both Border Collie and owner.

The answer to the question posed in the title is, "Probably not." The characteristics required of a Border Collie owner are complex and uncommon.

Lifestyles

City Dwellers with Border Collies

Border Collies can live well in the city given plenty of exercise, something to do, plenty of attention, and a lot of time. If you live in the city and are exploring the possibility of getting a Border Collie, ask yourself the following questions:

1. How much are you home?

2. Does your job require you to travel with any frequency?

Border Collies make excellent pets and companions if, and only if, you fit their needs.

3. What do you enjoy doing in your free time?

4. Are there facilities close to your home for exercising your pet?

5. Do you have the interest and the time to engage in Obedience, Agility, or other forms of training?

The questions listed above are measures of the time you have, and are willing to spend, with your Border Collie. You do not have to sacrifice your social life, abandon your spouse, or give up other interests to own a Border Collie, but you will have to make adjustments.

✔ If you live alone and travel as a regular part of your job, consider another breed.

✔ If you do not live within easy commuting range of Obedience classes, jogging tracks, and/or a park, maybe some other dog will serve you better.

✔ Finally, if you would rather spend time at a sports bar, a concert, or an athletic event than working your Border Collie, do yourself a favor and buy a stuffed dog.

✔ If you cannot be home at a predictable hour, Border Collies are not for you. For that matter, if you cannot make it home at a predictable hour, no breed is really for you.

Border Collies in the Suburbs

Suburbanites have to ask themselves the same questions about their time and their willingness to share it with a Border Collie. Living in the suburbs may have the disadvantage of a longer commute to work, providing less time for you to spend with your Border Collie. There may be offsetting advantages in the easy availability of veterinary services, places to exercise your Border Collie, and the accessibility of Obedience classes and trials. Similarly, suburban life will offer the choice of keeping your Border Collie in the house, in the yard, or some combination of the two.

If you do live in the suburbs, consider the neighbors. Most suburban areas are relatively lax in their control of dogs. Border Collies are not especially prone to barking but they are dogs and may bark excessively if particularly bored. Make sure your neighbors will not be offended by the occasional bout of barking or cat chasing. Most bad habits such as barking and cat chasing can be cured, but they have to happen before they can be cured. Make sure your neighbor is a dog lover, has no special health problems, and will be tolerant of a new dog.

More important, you will have to do everything in your power to make sure that your Border Collie will not be a nuisance to the neighborhood. He should be in his own yard at all times when he is not on a leash. A well-bred, handsome Border Collie tunneling through a flower bed is no more acceptable to your neighbor than having a mangy half-breed do the same thing.

To make your dog happier in the suburbs, consider providing your Border Collie with the following:

✔ A yard fenced with wiring that is escape-proof.

✔ A play area for your Border Collie that will allow him to dig to his heart's content. Sandboxes are made for this.

✔ A yard cleared of the toxic plants and other safety hazards that could cause your pet harm (see page 87 for a list of toxic plants).

✔ A supply of toys for your Border Collie in his play area. This will not only give him something to do, it will help keep him out of trouble in other areas of the yard.

✔ Constant antichasing training. Discourage Fleet from chasing the neighborhood cats. It will keep him from getting in bad with your neighbors and it could well save him injury or death if he ever escapes your yard.

Country Border Collies

Even if you live in the country you may not be Border Collie material. The questions asked of the city dweller apply to people from the country too. Do you have the time to devote to a Border Collie? If you live in the country and commute to the city to work, you may not be in any better shape than the suburbanite or city dweller.

Obviously, cattle and sheep ranchers have a use for Border Collies. Exercise is typically not an issue on a ranch.

Housing: Housing will be an issue, even in the country. The country Border Collie will need the same dry, draft-proof housing as its suburban or city cousins. For the country dog, the outside kennel is more practical than other forms of housing. True, Border Collies can live in country homes as well as they can live in urban apartments. Problems may arise in the country because country Border Collies, particularly working dogs, regularly come in contact with substances most homeowners do not want in their houses. The outside kennel offers warmth, protection from the elements, and a high level of sanitation.

Grooming: Another issue that may be even more important for the country Border Collie than those in the city or the suburbs is grooming. Working dogs and those nonworking Border Collies that are often in fields and forests are exposed to the burrs and briars that grow there. These briars and burrs cause matting if they are not removed as quickly as possible. The regular grooming recommended for the city is even more important for the country Border Collie. Rough-coated Border Collies are especially at risk.

Border Collies with Children

Having been bred for centuries to "look to" humans, it is not surprising that aggression toward people is rare in the breed. That is not to say that the odd Border Collie cannot be bad-tempered or aggressive, just that such dogs are much harder to find than in some other breeds. Given the appropriate training, Border Collies are ideal for children.

Older dogs have an advantage over puppies and younger dogs. They are calmer, typically more experienced with a wider range of people, and more tolerant of the bizarre ranges of behavior that humans can exhibit.

Young Border Collies, on the other hand, have nothing to work on except energy, herding

The young Border Collie's energy and enthusiasm make it a favorite with children.

instinct, and intelligence. They are more than willing to play with children and can delight entire neighborhoods. However, the herding instinct tells them that it is perfectly acceptable to nip whatever they are trying to herd. It is

TIP

Supervising Your New Border Collie

When introducing a young Border Collie into your home, be certain that someone has an eye on the new dog all the time. If your new dog harms or harasses any of your other pets, he must be corrected immediately. Socialization must begin at once and continue for the dog's life. Once the animal comes to learn that other pets are part of the environment, he will accept them readily.

One of the best ways to keep down friction between a Border Collie and a cat is to introduce them early in their lives.

hard for a toddler to accept the fact that the painful little nips are not malicious.

Starting as early in their life as possible, young dogs should be trained not to herd anything other than stock. Even then, they should work only on command. When a Border Collie attempts to "herd" something he should not, he must be corrected as quickly as possible. If, for instance, your Border Collie tries to bunch the neighbor's children, stop him and shout "*NO!*" Any time the behavior occurs again, let him know that you are displeased. It should not take long for him to learn what to work, and when.

Possible Problems with Other Pets

Because Border Collies are unique dogs, they offer unique problems. A Border Collie around cats or other pets can be something of a problem. The inbred herding instinct may pop to the surface around cats, ducks, rabbits, or other small animals. Ducks, rabbits, and other pets may be put into some danger if a young dog is allowed to move them around in hot weather.

Cats

Some dogs may choose to chase cats. This may not seem like much of a threat considering the number of cats chased every day, but Border Collies are a little faster than most breeds of dogs. Even given an exceptional start, most cats will have a problem escaping from a young, excited Border Collie. It is rare, even when the Border Collie catches the cat, that any real damage is done. About the only real damage that is likely to be done is to the relationship between you and the cat's owner. This is another area of focus for training.

A mixed breed and a Border Collie hit it off well, but puppies always get along.

Finding a Border Collie

As the Border Collie's popularity has grown in recent years, it has become progressively easier to find them. Finding a Border Collie 30 years ago required focused detective work unless you were already in touch with Border Collie people. Today it is almost impossible to open a newspaper, an agricultural bulletin, or shopper's guide without encountering at least one Border Collie for sale.

Where should you go to find a Border Collie? There is a simple answer to this question. Find a farmer, or a rancher, or someone else who has a litter of Border Collie puppies from working stock and buy one. An adult Border Collie from working stock will serve just as well if he has not been spoiled in some way.

Obedience handlers frequently have more than one breed of dog. Usually, they buy new dogs, Border Collies or otherwise, and rarely breed them. It is the farmer, the rancher, or the trialing enthusiast who will be more prone to breed quality Border Collies. Time spent driving to a ranch or farm to look over puppies is time well invested. If ranchers and/or farmers in the region do not have puppies, most of the registries and clubs listed in the back of this book will provide lists of members in your area. They will not, of course, recommend one breeder over another, but they will provide a list of members. Some maintain lists of members who breed their Border Collies. These lists are provided free or at low cost.

CHOOSING A BORDER COLLIE

Although people speak of Border Collies as if they were all the same, there are some differences from dog to dog. True they are active, curious, intelligent, and highly loyal as a breed, but depending upon bloodlines and previous experiences, there can be startling differences.

Selecting the Right Border Collie

Aside from the few physical and psychological characteristics that make Border Collies unique, the individuals in the breed vary widely. Some Border Collies are aggressive and confident; others are shy and withdrawn. If you choose to go with an adult Border Collie, be certain that you understand his personality and that he is compatible with your needs. A shy dog will not fit the needs of a cattle rancher but may be an excellent house pet and companion.

Adult Border Collies

Depending upon how they have been treated in their lives, adult Border Collies may bring a great deal of baggage with them when they

Note the physical differences between the standing female and the reclining male.

arrive. Caring, careful masters have raised most adult Border Collies, but as such things happen, sometimes the fondest owner must find a new home for his or her pets when changes occur in his or her life.

Unfortunately, some Border Collies have not been well used. Abused or ignored dogs will have difficulty trusting a new master. Worse, Border Collies that have been penned and ignored may never develop the intelligence that is their birthright.

Puppies

If you decide on a puppy, remember that puppies are nothing more than fur-covered potential. What they can become is already defined in their genetic structure. Of course, their ancestors contribute their genes by way of their parents, but the environment and treatment the puppy receives are also critical to the development of its unique personality.

Rescue centers can be excellent places to find adult Border Collies, if you can pass their criteria.

Advantages of Each

What are the advantages of an adult Border Collie over a puppy? Adult Border Collies have gone through the growing pains, puppy illnesses, house-training, and teething. They are what they will be, allowing for a little training.

Puppies have the advantage of being yours to mold. Border Collies will learn your idiosyncrasies as they mature. Their personality will develop as a function of your personality. Given the right puppy and intelligent, patient training, you will have the Border Collie you want.

Some professional trainers and handlers will not have a Border Collie unless they get it as a puppy, raise and train it themselves. Other equally successful trainers will seek out young adult Border Collies in preference to puppies. Which is better, adult or puppy? With careful selection, it probably does not matter.

Rescue Centers

If you do decide that an adult Border Collie is right for you, check local and regional rescue centers. These centers take in Border Collies that have been abandoned or must be placed because of changes in their owners' lives. Other Border Collies arrive at rescue facilities because the owner has discovered that he or she is not Border Collie material. These are dogs in need of homes, some of them desperately so. At rescue shelters they are given food, shelter, and as much training and love as possible. Some of the dogs arrive healthy and intact. Others, unfortunately, arrive neurotic and fearful of humans. It is the latter group that receives the lion's share of attention and training. Some rescue shelters have had incredible success rehabilitating these animals.

Rescue center personnel will know their dogs intimately. They have a reputation for being extremely honest and will expect the same of applicants for the Border Collies under their charge. Applications for dogs from rescue shelters are frequently more detailed than those required at dating services and job placement businesses.

Again, most of the registries and clubs listed in the back keep close contact with the local Border Collie rescue organizations. They are typically more than happy to provide information about Border Collie rescue centers in your area. If you are interested in a Border Collie from a rescue organization, you might try the National Directory of Rescuers USA and Canada at *http://bcrnd.org/id27.htm.*

Male or Female?

One of the major decisions in selecting a dog of any kind is gender. As in most breeds, there are advantages and disadvantages to both the male and the female. Males will tend to be a little larger, more aggressive, more headstrong, and generally more impressive in terms of looks. Females are typically smaller, more affectionate, less resistant to training, and a little more sensitive than males.

All the characteristics mentioned in the previous paragraph are tendencies. The statements are all true, generally. However, there are female Border Collies that are bigger than the average male Border Collie, while some male Border Collies are shyer and more sensitive than the general run of females.

Before you select a Border Collie, think about what you really want in a dog.

✔ Do you want an affectionate pet that will spend a great deal of time with its head in your lap?

✔ Are you easygoing, relatively soft-spoken?

✔ Do you have limited space in which to house your Border Collie?

If you answered, "yes" to all, or any of these questions, you might best consider a female Border Collie or another breed.

✔ Do you need a strong dog for working stock?

✔ Are you loud spoken or abrupt in your movements?

✔ Do you just like the larger, nobler-looking male Border Collie?

Consider a male Border Collie as your first choice.

Male Border Collies tend to be larger, a little more aggressive, and slightly more headstrong than females.

Neutering

Again, there is an enormous overlap in Border Collie characteristics. Do not go into the selection process with your decision already made. There is only one thing that is absolute in selecting the sex of your Border Collie: All Border Collies should be neutered unless they have been obtained specifically for stock work and have excelled at that. By neutering your Border Collie, you will reduce or eliminate many of the problems associated with owning a dog.

✔ Neutered females will not attract suitors every six months. If you want a Border Collie for working stock, you definitely do not want stray dogs rambling among the flock twice a year.

✔ Neutering also eliminates unwanted mixed-breed litters and the resultant drain on the female.

✔ Neutered males will not try to escape from your kennel or yard to go courting. It is likely that more Border Collie males are killed every year trying to reach a female in heat than for any other reason.

✔ If your male Border Collie does not particularly care who is in heat, he will be less likely to go AWOL and wander under the wheels of a moving eighteen-wheeler.

✔ The final reason for neutering is to take all but the best Border Collies out of the gene pool. Border Collies with overbites, bad hips, or other defects should be removed from the breeding population when the defect is discovered, no matter what the original reason for purchase.

Working Stock?

One decision you will have to make is whether to obtain a Border Collie from working stock rather than some other source. The simple answer to this question is "yes." Border Collies became Border Collies by working. The characteristics of intelligence, athleticism, and willingness to learn have developed as necessary secondary characteristics for the working dog. A Border Collie from other than working stock will be less likely to have these characteristics than working stock will. Puppies from farms, ranches, and/or trial stock are preferable to Border Collies from stock that has never worked. Be sure that the parents have been X-rayed and found free of hip dysplasia, and that DNA test or examination by a canine ophthalmologist to assure that your Border Collie is free of Collie Eye Anomaly (see page 73). Your chances of getting a healthy, intelligent puppy increase dramatically by following these guidelines. Remember, no matter where you get your Border Collie, *all* are high-energy creatures. There is no such thing as a lazy Border Collie unless it is sick or very old.

For purchase of a puppy, working stock is always the best choice.

Which Puppy of the Litter?

If you have set your mind on a Border Collie puppy and have located a likely litter from working stock, you still have to select a single puppy from that litter. That selection is not easy. Healthy Border Collie puppies are uniformly adorable. At the age of six or eight weeks they tend to be cute, furry, and rambunctious. Selecting one puppy out of the litter is like selecting the best dish at a great restaurant.

TIP

Selecting a Puppy

At the age of six to eight weeks there is very little way to tell how a puppy will turn out. Just find a good litter of healthy puppies and pick one.

American handlers will frequently give the opinion that a buyer should select the first puppy that runs up to them. Most buyers will select the friendliest or handsomest puppy of a litter. One of the best-known handlers and trainers of Border Collies in Britain has suggested that the prospective buyer should take the puppy that hangs back to watch. It is his contention that the puppy that sits and observes is the only one of the litter with the brains to know that you are a stranger.

Best Way to Select

What then is the best way to select a good Border Collie puppy? There is no best way. If you have found a good, healthy litter from working stock, just close your eyes and pick a puppy. If you have determined that you need a male or a female, divide the litter by sex and grab a puppy from the male or female group. If you really feel that a smooth-haired puppy best fits your needs, select a smooth-haired puppy. If you want a handsome puppy, select the handsomest of the lot.

A Few Musts in Buying a Border Collie

✔ Check up on the breeder. Make sure the breeder's puppies are genetically sound, well cared for, and have received all their inoculations. You may get a few negative readings even if the breeder is solid. Some of this is probably due to unrealistically high expectations of the breed. The trick is to find enough people with experience with the breeder that you get a true reading for him or her.
✔ Visit the breeder's kennels. Most of the undesirable things about a dog kennel can be spotted quickly. If you see uncleaned kennels, dirty pans, or water bowls without water, it is time to look elsewhere.
✔ If you find a breeder with a puppy you like, arrange with the breeder to take the puppy to a veterinarian and a canine ophthalmologist. Having both professionals examine the puppy will ensure healthy body and eyes.
✔ It is not unreasonable for some sort of deposit to be left with the breeder pending the examination(s).
✔ If your breeder of choice refuses independent examination, move on to another breeder.

Health Contract

Since a number of canine illnesses do not appear until well into the first year, a good breeder will offer you a guarantee of health as part of a standard purchase. This health contract will give the buyer the option of returning the young dog if some illness arises.

Other Information

There should also be suggestions on diet, genetic information, if provided by the seller, and registration information.

Getting Your New Border Collie Home

If you have settled on an adult Border Collie, getting him to your home should be somewhat easier than a puppy, especially if the adult dog has been acquired through an adoption agency or humane shelter where extra attention and training are standard. Adult dogs can be put into shipping crates, comforted, and the journey home begun.

Which puppy of the litter? Not the brown and white, wooly one. Other than that, all things being equal, pick the one you like best.

Puppies, on the other hand, are new to the world and need some extra support. Puppies should also be put in a shipping crate with adequate padding and a chew toy. Proceed as directly as possible to your residence. Anything you need for your new Border Collie should be on hand before he is picked up.

In the event that the puppy is to be a resident of the house, the crate can be used for his doghouse-in-the-house after the trip. It is probably best to have someone along for the trip to help keep an eye on the new Border Collie.

A good supply of food and water should be supplied. Frequent rest, exercise, and "pit stops" are highly recommended.

Note: Under no circumstances should you put a Border Collie puppy on the floorboard or on someone's lap.

A Word of Caution: Puppy Mills

When the puppy mill operator is able to distance himself from his market, greater dangers arise for the potential buyer. Such dumping places for puppy mills include Internet dealers and some pet stores. While some of these places may be perfectly upright, it is quicker and easier to go with a proven breeder, a rescue organization, or a humane shelter.

LIVING WITH A BORDER COLLIE

Living with Border Collies offers challenges that other breeds do not. While terriers are proven diggers, the Belgian breeds are highly intelligent, and Greyhounds extremely active, Border Collies offer the whole package. It can be highly positive or highly negative, depending on training, exercise, and the environment.

Keeping a Border Collie in Your Yard

A fenced yard is a good place to keep your Border Collie. If properly built, the fence will offer some of the benefits of a kennel with more room to move around. Many Border Collies live happily in a standard chain-link fenced yard; other Border Collies do not even slow down when they encounter a 4-foot (122 cm) chain-link fence, and some Border Collies will tunnel under fences with the same enthusiasm that they work sheep or run Agility courses. If you plan to keep your Border Collie in a fenced yard, be sure to have an alternate plan.

Owning a Border Collie entails a great deal of forethought. This smooth-coated Border Collie seems to be doing a little looking ahead itself.

Digging

Even those Border Collies that stay in a fenced yard can offer problems. The same digging that creates problems with containing the dogs can also create problems in the garden, the yard, and in flower beds. If you happen to catch your Border Collie digging where he should not, correct him immediately. A loud *"No"* will let him know that he has done something wrong. You should also protect areas of your yard and garden if you buy a young Border Collie.

Safety

Keeping your Border Collie in the yard presents a number of safety problems. Over time, many homes create hazards they don't even realize until a dog arrives. Pesticides are common problems; there are a number of toxic

6

Flowerbeds are another area that the family should work together to keep the Border Collie out of.

Some Border Collies can be difficult to keep in a standard chain link fence. Consider the height of this Border Collie over an Agility hurdle.

garden plants (see page 87) that can cause problems ranging from stomach problems to death.

Border Collies in the House

Keeping Border Collies in the house poses some of the same problems as keeping them in the yard:

1. First, the house has to be Border Collie-proofed; potential dangers for your dog will have to be searched out and removed. Remember that because your dog will have a different point of view regarding your house, literally.

2. An adult Border Collie's head will be no more than 2 feet (60 cm) off the floor. He will

see things that you miss from your vantage point. In your search for electric wires, sharp objects, and potential poisons, sit or lie on the floor. You may feel a little silly, but what you see from your prone position may save your Border Collie's life.

3. Next, your dog will have to have a place of his own. At the very least, he should have an area with a bed and a place to keep his toys. He should be taught that the area is his.

4. He should be taught that certain areas of the house are off limits. If your Border Collie wanders into forbidden territory, he should be corrected immediately. A few loud "*No's*" will have the new dog dodging couches and detouring around dining rooms.

In order for the restriction training to work, everyone in the house will have to know about it and support it.

Crate Training

Your Border Collie needs to be crate-trained if he is to live in your house—in fact, *all* Border Collies should be crate-trained. Inside dogs can use the crate daily but all dogs should be trained to stay in an air kennel or wire kennel of some sort. Crate training will get your dog accustomed to being confined, which has benefits for both of you: your Border Collie gets a safe place to spend his off time and you get a dog that does not mind being closed up in a crate or wire kennel. So, when you have guests that do not like dogs, or guests that your dog does not like, he may be put into his crate for a while.

Travel: Crate training will make travel with your dog a great deal easier. Taking a piece of home along with you in the car or the motel room will make your dog more comfortable.

What and When to Feed Your Border Collie

It is best to feed a new Border Collie whatever he was eating before he came home with you, no matter how much you would prefer a different food for him. This is especially true if the new dog is to live in the house. An abrupt change in diet can result in diarrhea, not something that is popular in most households. Talk to your veterinarian about a good feed for your Border Collie at his age. If it is not the same feed he is eating at that moment, gradually phase in the new feed until the old food is no longer used.

Scraps

Avoid feeding the puppy table scraps. Table scraps are just the thing for getting your puppy fat, giving him diarrhea, or constipating him.

A wire crate or air kennel is an ideal time out for your Border Collie. Because you will be taking its bedroom with you, travel becomes a little easier, too.

Table scraps cannot possibly supply the vitamins, minerals, protein, and fat that a high-quality puppy food can provide.

How Often?

Puppies under eight weeks of age should be fed three or four times a day. From eight weeks to six months, three times a day, and thereafter, twice a day. Until your Border Collie reaches a year old, he should be fed a good-quality puppy food. He might look like an adult, but he will be a puppy at least until 12 months of age.

Border Collies should be fed in the same place whenever possible. However, these red merle puppies don't seem to mind not eating at home.

How Much?

Border Collie puppies do not need to be as fat as most owners like. Overeating and overweight are major contributors to hip dysplasia, a problem with the ball sockets, so more than one canine nutritionist has suggested that you feed dogs of all ages, Border Collies included, about 25 percent less than the amount suggested by the manufacturer (see page 43, Nutrition).

Border Collie Equipment

Collars

All Border Collies will need a collar and a leash immediately upon arriving at their new home. Have a new collar fitted so that you can get one finger between the dog's neck and the collar. Day-to-day collars are available in nylon, cotton, and leather. Your Border Collie should have a collar with an ID tag that provides your name, address, and telephone number; you can also include your dog's name. The collar also includes a handy place to hang the Border Collie's most current rabies tags, a requirement in most jurisdictions.

Training Collars

A second type of collar will be necessary when you begin training your Border Collie for Obedience. These collars are most commonly referred to as "choke collars." Training collars are not used to restrict air intake in the trainee, but to correct him when he does not respond immediately to a command. You will find that training collars are available in a variety of sizes and qualities. Buy the heaviest, best-made collar you can afford—you will not need one of the training collars with spikes on the inside; Border Collies learn quickly that such a collar is painful. They will also learn that Obedience sessions are to be avoided if you use such a collar. Stick to the standard stainless steel or chrome collar in the correct weight for your Border Collie.

Tattoos and Microchips

You can have your Border Collie tattooed in an inconspicuous place so he can be identified if he gets lost.

If you wish, you can have him chipped. A microchip can be inserted under his skin with a hypodermic needle. If your Border Collie is stolen or wanders and is recovered by a local pound or humane shelter, he can be identified by a simple wave of an electronic wand.

Remember when you put the training collar on your Border Collie that there is a right and wrong way to perform this simple task. The collar will have a ring at each end. A loop is formed with the collar by looping it through one of the rings. One ring will have the chain of the collar passing through it; the other will be clear. It is the ring through which no chain passes that should have the leash attached to it. The free ring should be placed to the right side of the Border Collie's neck. All this placement information may sound trivial, but an ill-placed training collar can bind and choke the dog. It will take only one or two instances of choking for any dog's enthusiasm for training to wane a little.

The Leash

A good leash, another necessity, is critical to controlling and training a Border Collie. Like collars, they are made of leather, nylon, or cotton. Unlike collars, the first leash you buy for your Border Collie may well be the last if it is well constructed. You will also find some with leather or nylon handles, chain bodies, ring, and clip. Some trainers do not particularly like chain leashes because of the noise made by the links when the dogs move. Leashes typically will be about 6 feet (1.8 m) although some Obedience trainers like them much shorter. Talk to your Obedience trainer about his or her preferences.

Grooming Supplies

Border Collies are fortunate in that their fur is relatively dry and does not tangle easily. This is true of both the smooth- and the rough-haired varieties of the breed. Although the breed is low maintenance, at least compared to some other breeds, a regular regimen of groom-

Starting early with a grooming program makes it easier to become a normal part of your Border Collie's life.

ing is a necessity. Both coat types have a thick undercoat that can become tangled in the presence of dirt, brambles, and twigs.

✔ The basic hardware requirements for a complete Border Collie grooming session will include a good pair of scissors, a metal comb, a slicker brush, a pin brush, and a mat rake.

✔ Outside Border Collies will probably not need their nails clipped, but they should be checked regularly and trimmed as necessary, so good clippers are a necessity.

Invest a little extra in these items. Regular grooming, particularly if your Border Collie is an outside dog, can create a lot of wear and tear on grooming equipment; cheaper equipment will have to be replaced again and again. Better-made grooming equipment will hold up better,

sparing you the cost of replacement. For more information on grooming, see pages 33–38.

Toys

Border Collies have to understand that a natural chewing instinct cannot be directed at everything around them. Again, this is one of those situations where offering them alternatives to baseboards and draperies is better than trying to make them understand that the enormous hole in the couch is not acceptable, so have a good supply of dog toys available for your Border Collie. Let Fleet know what is his, what he can chew, and what he cannot. Keep the toys in the same place and available to your Border Collie at all times.

Balls: Good choices would be a ball small enough for your Border Collie to handle, but large enough that it will not get hung up in his throat. These balls are available in a number of materials, including rawhide.

Other toys that squeak, rattle, tinkle, and even talk are available to entertain the dogs in your house.

Border Collies in the house, in the yard, especially in the kennel, seem to like toys. This one seems to have a stuffed sheep, appropriately enough.

Chew Toys: Chew toys, like rawhide bones and beef bones are not toys but are excellent supplements to his collection. Coupled with a little discipline in keeping your shoes and other articles off the floor and out of sight, these toys can help keep your Border Collie, and you, happy as he adjusts to life with you. Having some approved toys to shake, toss, and chew helps keep stress to a minimum and helps keep gums healthy.

Note: It is important to have toys available to dogs that live outside; even they get bored and stressed and toys help them too.

The Outdoor Dog

The outside is an excellent place for Border Collies if you keep up an exercise program as you should for an inside dog. If you live in the suburbs, you will need an escape-proof fence, chain-link, for privacy. If you would rather have your Border Collie live in a kennel, check local building codes to determine what you can build.

Kennels

The country dog will definitely need a kennel. Most kennels are built on a 4-inch (10-cm) slab with a slight slope to the rear where there is a drainage depression. This will allow the owner to wash droppings out of the kennel, into the depression, out to a disposal system of some type.

Wire

There will need to be chain-link wire around these kennels; 6 feet (1.8 m) is a good height.

Border Collie puppies can relax anywhere.

Kennels should be at least 4 feet (1.22 m) by 8 feet (2.4 m); 6 feet (1.8 m) by 8 feet (2.4 m) is even better. They should be sprayed down daily.

The Doghouse

There are any number of commercially made doghouses available, mostly plastic. Better houses are made of wood and allow the dog to have his own den.

✔ The ideal doghouse should be raised 3 to 6 inches (7–15 cm) off the ground, which will protect the house from dampness and will cause it to be cooler in hot weather.

✔ The house should be built with a frame structure that has a slight slope to the rear of the roof.

✔ There should be two equal-sized chambers, divided by a partial wall. This wall should be made of 3/4-inch (19-mm) plywood and extend roughly three-quarters of the way across the chamber. The outside of the house should be made of half-inch (13-mm) plywood.

✔ The outside door should be roughly the same size as the inside chamber door.

✔ There should be a few inches of overlap in the roof to help keep the internal chambers dry.

✔ Of course, the outside walls should be painted and the roof shingled.

Size

Make the doghouse large enough that the Border Collie can stretch out full length with plenty of room left over.

Inside the Doghouse

In cooler weather the house should contain bedding, cedar shavings, or clean straw. Bedding material should be removed periodically, and replaced. If a bed is used, it should be washed, dried, and returned to its place. In some cases, the owner might want to consider hanging a flap of heavy canvas over one or both doors in the house. This cuts down on drafts and makes the house considerably warmer. Canvas should be available at local hardware or fabric stores.

GROOMING YOUR BORDER COLLIE

Due to the variety of hair coats in Border Collies, and the presence of a thick undercoat, regular, patient grooming is a must. If begun when the Border Collie is a puppy and done gently, it can easily become an enjoyable activity between owner and dog; handled poorly and the Border Collie may never accept grooming gracefully.

The Smooth-Haired Border Collie

Smooth-haired dogs have some advantage over their longer-haired brothers and sisters. The absence of "feathers" below the body and around the chest and legs reduces the likelihood that the smooth-haired dog will have mats. Grooming three or four times a week will reduce the probability to near zero.

Pin Brush

Begin grooming the smooth-haired dog with a pin brush. Start at the side of the dog's head and brush gently toward the tail. Except in cases where the coat is matted you should be

This rough-coated Border Collie has obviously seen his share of careful care and good grooming.

able to cover the entire body with the pin brush without stopping. If you do hit a mat, work around it. It does not do either of you any good to teach the dog that grooming is painful.

Steel Comb

When you have completed grooming your Border Collie, use a steel comb to brush the coat against the grain. On a smooth-haired Border Collie this will not have the impact that it will on the longer-haired variety, but it will remove any hair missed while brushing with the grain.

Try to divide the grooming process into segments. Make brushing separate and distinct from combing. Combing should also be distinguishable from removing mats and tangles. It might help the process if you give Fleet a treat between stages.

Smooth-coated Border Collies like this one are a little easier to groom than their rough-coated brothers and sisters. But they still need a regular schedule of grooming.

The Rough-Haired Border Collie

The only real difference in grooming rough-haired Border Collies and smooth-haired Border Collies is that rough-haired dogs have longer guard hairs and "feathers" on the back of their legs and chest. The fine undercoat present in smooth-haired dogs is also present in their rougher-haired siblings. The longer guard hairs require that the fur be groomed in layers. Longer hair will also mat more readily than smooth hair. Mat removal becomes more important if you own a rough-haired Border Collie.

Pin Brush

Start with the pin brush. Brush from the side of the head to the base of the tail. Work from the side of the head where you originally started, around the head, back to the place you started.

Metal Comb

When you have successfully brushed the entire surface area of the dog with the grain, use a metal comb. Be cautious while combing and brushing. If you encounter tangles or mats, move around them to come back later. Use the same techniques to remove mats as for smooth-haired dogs. You will find the mat rake even more useful with the rough-haired dogs.

Every effort should be made to make grooming pleasant. Incorporate basic grooming while petting your dog. A pin brush may be used to scratch behind a dog's ear as effectively as fingers.

Professionals

Finally, if you are not confidant in your ability to groom your Border Collie well, consider a professional groomer. Search for a groomer with a good reputation, an easy manner with the dogs, and a clean shop. Check with local interest groups, Obedience clubs, and acquaintances for references; go door-to-door if need be. Professionals do not have to be expensive, just enthusiastic and clean.

Ears

Border Collies' ears should be examined regularly since they are particularly attractive to ticks and ear mites. When either of these parasites is found, appropriate treatment should be given.

Your Border Collie's ears should also be examined regularly for damage. While Border Collies are not as aggressive as some other breeds, they will occasionally get into fights that can produce cuts and abrasions on ears. They are also extremely active animals and are frequently worked in rough country. Scratches, scrapes, and tears from briars and rough undergrowth are common on the external ears. These wounds should be treated with local antiseptic.

TIP

Mats and Tangles

The least stressful way to remove mats is to split them with your fingers first.

✔ Grab the mat as close to the skin as possible and pull apart gently. If the mat is especially large or compacted, or if it has sticks or briars in the center, it may not split easily.

✔ Hold the mat close to the skin with a comb or mat rake and try to pull it apart. Take special care not to hurt your dog.

✔ If the dog becomes edgy or tense, move on to another mat or take a short break.

✔ Take your time, move slowly, and try to make the experience as positive as possible for your dog.

✔ If the mat proves resistant to fingers and the mat rake, use grooming scissors to split it—here, again, investing in a good pair of scissors is important. Do not use household scissors. Household scissors are too long. The tips of household scissors can wind up in a dog's eye or an ear may be shortened by accident. Use the scissors as a last resort.

If the wounds are severe, take your dog to a veterinarian for treatment.

The ear canal and underside of the external ear should be cleaned as a regular part of your Border Collie's grooming. A greasy, sometimes smelly, black substance will build up on the inside of the external ear, close to the head. Use a cotton swab to clean the grooves and crevasses of this black matter.

A Border Collie showing "eye," even though no livestock is present.

to be safe, Border Collies' feet should be examined regularly. Cuts should be treated immediately since they can lead to infections and greater problems. Sharp objects, scrap metal, and glass should be removed from your pet's environment. Anything that can be done to prevent foot damage should be done.

Puppies

Border Collie puppies, on the other hand, should have their nails trimmed regularly, beginning at an early age. Special care should be taken with dewclaws.

The quick: When trimming, stay clear of the quick. The quick is the only part of the nail with nerves and blood vessels. "Quicking" not only produces blood; it hurts. If your Border Collie associates nail-trimming with pain, the next nail-trimming session will be extremely difficult, so be careful!

Caution: Always keep the head of the swab in sight as you clean around the entrance to the ear canal.

Dirt and gunk from the external ear can be packed into the ear canal, increasing the possibility of ear infection. If you think the ear canal needs to be cleaned, ask your veterinarian to take a look at it.

Feet and Nails

As mentioned previously, Border Collies are active dogs and do not typically need their nails trimmed as often as most breeds. However, just

The Anal Glands

One of the most unpleasant duties any dog owner will ever have to perform is checking the anal glands. These are a pair of glands at about five o'clock and seven o'clock just inside the dog's anus. The glands themselves are about the size of a kidney bean with a short outlet to the anus. When these outlets become impacted and/or the glands become infected, problems can occur. Tipoffs can be when a dog licks his anus much more than usual, turns around and around as if he is trying to catch the base of his tail, or scoots along on his rear through grass or along carpet.

Rough-coated Border Collies require more grooming for prime coat condition, but some owners think it is worth the effort.

Scooting: Please understand that if the Border Collie is suffering enough discomfort at this point to scoot around, best get him outside.

Odor: Frequently, along with the scooting comes one of the most atrocious smells dogs can produce.

The Groomer or Veterinarian

Even though cleaning the glands is a relatively easy task, some owners are not comfortable doing it themselves. No matter who does it, as soon as your dog shows these signs, have your veterinarian or your groomer do it. If the problem is chronic, ask someone who knows the procedure to show you how so the trips to the veterinarian or groomer will not be so regular. In some extreme cases, your veterinarian may have to treat an extreme infection with antibiotics.

Under most circumstances the anal gland does not have to be cleaned or emptied; natural pressure from bowel movements will empty the glands normally, so regular cleaning of healthy anal glands is not only unnecessary but can actually be harmful. Keep an eye on your Border Collie, but do not overdo care in this area.

Persistent Odors

Like all dogs, Border Collies are prone to roll in manure, dead things, and things too horrible to mention. It has been speculated that since wolves did not have the capability of returning to the den area and explaining to their pack-mates that they had discovered a winter-killed elk somewhere back up in the hills, one or more of the wolves would roll in the carrion and take

Any Border Collie would smell sweet in these flowers, but in real life they can get into some really foul-smelling messes.

the odor back to the pack. It may have worked well enough for wolves, but it has its limitations for housedogs. More than one surprised owner has had an excited dog romp into the house reeking of something dead. Country dogs can get a double dose of smell and color by rolling in fresh manure.

Shampoo

The first-best option, and occasionally, second-best option is to bathe your Border Collie in a strong dog shampoo. Your veterinarian, groomer, or local pet spa can typically provide the best type. Do not use liquid cleaner, human shampoo, or dishwashing liquid as such liquids can dry out your dog's hair. Bathing the dog, allowing him to dry, bathing him again, allow-

ing him to dry, and grooming him will take care of all but the most stubborn odors.

Skunks

But what if your dog gets "skunked"? You had better hope you have some place to keep him outside; it is better that his kennel or doghouse gets a little smelly than your house. It may take two or three weeks for the smell to go away, even if you take action.

Teeth

Along with regular physical exams, your Border Collie should be scheduled for dental exams at least annually. If your veterinarian suggests professional cleaning (under anesthesia), have

CHECKLIST

Removing Skunk Odor

1. Check for eye irritation. If your Border Collie paws at his eyes, or has red eyes, relieve the irritation with nonprescription eyedrops or olive oil.

2. Put on a pair of rubber gloves and use a dog shampoo to wash the sprayed dog.

3. While the dog dries a little, take a trip to the grocery store for several cans of tomato juice—do not bother buying the best. Remember, you will be pouring it over a smelly dog.

4. When you get home, pour enough tomato juice on the dog to soak its coat through. Let it dry for about 30 minutes and wash it out.

5. Let the dog dry a little while, then soak with tomato juice again. Let it dry another half-hour, rinse, and let dry.

6. Hopefully, the skunk odor should be at least tolerable. You will probably have to shampoo more than once after this to get the odor completely out of your Border Collie's fur.

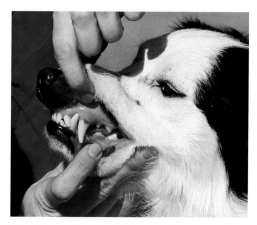

Checking a Border Collie's teeth is a regular part of bench trials, and it is an activity that all Border Collie owners should perform weekly.

✔ Provide veterinary approved chew toys. These toys are designed to enhance canine dental health.

✔ Feed kibbled foods; hard foods help reduce plaque buildup on teeth.

✔ Clean teeth several times a week with brushes and toothpaste especially developed for dogs. If the dog does not like brushes, you can clean his teeth by wrapping a thin cloth around your forefinger and using that instead.

✔ Begin cleaning your Border Collie's teeth as early as possible. Make the experience as pleasant as possible.

✔ Pull the gums away from the teeth and brush slowly up and down, taking care not to bruise the gums or lips. Work from the back of the mouth to the front, top to bottom. Once the outsides of the teeth have been cleaned, use the same techniques to clean the inside. You may find it necessary to take rest periods if your dog gets restless or upset.

it done. Buildup of tartar on the teeth is the number one cause of tooth disease and loss of teeth. The time and effort involved in getting your dog in for a dental appointment will pay off in the long run.

In between dental appointments:

✔ Check your pet's teeth regularly for decay, tartar, damage, and inclusions such as wood or other foreign substances.

NUTRITION

Canine nutrition has improved dramatically in recent years. Even mediocre feeds can provide excellent, broad-based nutrition. Especially formulated products are available for puppies, adults, and older dogs at affordable prices so that dogs can live healthier, longer lives.

Dietary Requirements

Feeding your Border Collie is a combination of tightrope walking and consistency. All dogs have minimum and maximum requirements for their dietary needs. Protein, fats, and carbohydrates make up the bulk of dog foods and must be present in the correct proportions. Minerals such as calcium and phosphorous are also necessary as are the multitude of vitamins that can cause confusion in human diets. If your Border Collie does not get the correct amounts of all the nutritional components, he will be something less than he could be. In extreme instances, diets that lacked vital nutritional elements have resulted in Border Collies that were deficient mentally.

Protein

When most people think of dietary requirements for dogs, they think of protein. While it is true that wild canids and feral dogs are car-

Good nutrition, good care, and plenty of exercise have kept this Border Collie alert at age 12.

nivores, their diets also include things other than meat. Feral and wild canids do kill and eat other animals, but they eat all of the animals they kill. If you have ever chanced upon a fresh dog or coyote kill, you may have noticed that the first things eaten in such kills are the intestines and their contents. By eating the contents of the intestines, the canids get a rich supply of vegetable matter and some enzymes that they cannot produce themselves. The point here is that dogs in their natural state do not eat an all-meat diet; it is liberally supplemented with vegetable matter.

Sources: Commercial dog food manufacturers include protein from a variety of sources including soybean meal, horsemeat, beef, chicken, fishmeal, and various combinations of "processed" parts and leftovers. Of course, meat and fish-based protein sources are digested more easily than plant-based sources. Kibble most commonly uses grain and soybean sources, semi-moist foods are typically soybean based, while canned foods are entirely meat or meat and grain combinations.

Border Collies burn more energy than most dogs, so they need a higher percentage of carbohydrates in their rations than the average dog.

Need: All dogs—Border Collies are no exception—require protein for growth, normal body maintenance, hair production, and as building blocks for healing after injuries. Puppies and pregnant females require higher levels of protein than adult and older dogs.

There is great controversy about how much protein is required, the protein source(s), and how protein should be distributed over a dog's life.

Carbohydrates

Carbohydrates are a source of energy in dog foods. Typically, carbohydrates in dog foods are derived from grain sources such as wheat or corn. The energy from carbohydrates is not as readily available to your dog as the energy from fats since it requires a more complex digestive process. It is from carbohydrates and fats that your Border Collie will derive all of his energy at the cellular level.

Fats

Dogs need, and can use, much more fat in their diets than humans. High-fat foods are generally more appealing to dogs than low-fat products. Humans, too, find the taste of fat and fat-based foods more appealing than their low- or no-fat equivalents. (If you doubt this, compare the taste of a regular potato chip against the taste of a baked chip.)

Your Border Collie will need minimum amounts of fat to maintain a healthy coat, a normally functioning neural system, and as a delivery medium for fat-soluble vitamins.

The downside to this is that fats, while easily converted into energy in active dogs, are just as easily converted into body fats in less active pets. You and your veterinarian need to monitor the body fat of your Border Collie and either adjust his activity level or his fat intake.

Vitamins

Most premium dog foods contain all of the minimum daily requirements of vitamins for your Border Collie, but in rare instances some supplements may be required. Vitamins, in the correct amounts and proportions, are absolutely necessary. When the amounts are not correct or the proportions are not in balance, your Border Collie may be harmed. Growing puppies are particularly subject to problems related to vitamin overdose. Discuss this with your veterinarian.

Minerals

Minerals are another dietary essential that can be overdone. Generally, all minerals required by your Border Collie will be present in a good-quality food. Find a food that meets your dog's needs and stick with it—or use a food recommended by your breeder or veterinarian.

The Effects of Good Early Nutrition

Puppy nutrition begins with feeding practices.

✔ Puppies should be fed from a bowl that can be cleaned easily.

✔ If they are to be fed in the house, they should be fed in a quiet, out-of-the-way area.

✔ They should be fed four times daily at the same time for each meal.

✔ When they reach three months, feedings should be cut back to three times daily, then to twice daily.

✔ At one year of age, puppies may be fed once daily.

The Growing Puppy

Your Border Collie puppy will continue to grow until he is 18 months to two years old. Since the puppy will be as tall as he will ever be at age nine months to one year, there is a tendency to assume he is full-grown. While that assumption does no real damage, feeding an immature dog as if he were an adult can.

Except for pregnant females, puppies need more protein than other dogs. A premium-quality puppy food will generally provide sufficient protein. Even puppies that grow as fast as Border Collies can get what they need from commercial foods. Recently, there has been some dispute as to how long immature Border Collies should be

It is difficult to tell without feeling this Border Collie puppy's pelvis and first rib, but it appears to be about the right weight.

TIP

Puppies' Feeding

If there is more than one puppy to be fed, they should be fed separately in order to better monitor each puppy's food intake.

More importantly, separate feeding prevents stronger puppies from getting all the food and the smaller ones from starving.

This Border Collie puppy is eating from a ceramic bowl that can be washed and cleaned easily.

kept on puppy food. Manufacturers recommend that growing dogs be kept on puppy food for a full year. In contrast, some canine nutritionists feel that puppies should be changed to adult dog food at age three months. The first recommendation may be based on the belief that when dogs eat puppy food for 12 months, the dog food company will sell more puppy food. The second recommendation is based on a belief that too much protein in a puppy's diet can result in such problems as osteochondritis desicans (see page 72). A diet too low in protein can produce an adult Border Collie that is less than he could have been, both physically and mentally.

What Is Different About Border Collie Nutrition?

There are two big differences between Border Collies and some collective prototype of all other dogs in the matter of nutrition.

This Border Collie puppy is eating from a ceramic bowl that can be washed and cleaned easily.

Big eaters: The first difference is that Border Collies are not normally big eaters. After the glutton stage that all dogs go through as puppies, they will tend to be thrifty eaters. Even the rare Border Collie that does eat large amounts of food, will tend to eat a little here, a little there. First-time Border Collie owners may be tempted to add treats to their dog's diet or even change foods. Unless there is some other reason to think that your Border Collie is not getting enough to eat, do not bother.

Size: Remember, Border Collies are supposed to be tuck-waisted. A Border Collie in excellent physical condition will invariably appear skinny, at least when he is wet. If your Border Collie is passing a veterinarian's examination, has normal energy for a Border Collie, and does eat, do not worry about playing musical dog foods.

Energy: Border Collies operate at full throttle for most of their waking time. As a result, they generally require a higher-energy food than most other breeds. Energy is provided in most dog foods in the form of fat. The more fat in a dog food, the more potential energy is available to the dog. But if that fat energy is not burned, it turns to puppy fat. Keep a close eye on the puppy's weight.

Labels

The proportions of fat and protein contained in a dog food are typically printed boldly on the label or the outside of the bag. At the very least, a federally required label will provide the nutritional breakdown of the product it represents.

Fat percentages in most dog foods will range from 8 percent to 15 percent, rarely higher. Most active Border Collies can make it on a feed with 12 percent fat. If your dog begins to lose weight or just runs out of juice during a normal workday, you have two options: You either need to up his ration of feed or change to a feed with a higher percentage of fat.

Commercial Diets—Pros and Cons

In the dog food section of your local supermarket you can find dry dog food, canned dog food, semisoft dog food, and even frozen dog food. There are gourmet foods, hypoallergenic foods, all-beef foods, all-chicken foods, all-turkey foods, and foods with mixtures of meats and vegetables. You will also find multicolored kibble, kibble in interesting shapes, and kibble with shapes that do not have any real reason for existence. Some commercial semisoft food looks like chunks of raw meat, some of the canned food looks like your Aunt Martha's beef stew, and some canned dog food looks as if the dog has already eaten it once.

Before you get too tangled up in the dog food marketing dilemma, there are several things you should remember:

1. Dogs are red/green color-blind—dog food could well be fuchsia and the dog would not know.

2. Your Border Collie has probably never been to dinner at your Aunt Martha's and has no idea what her beef stew looks like.

3. Few dogs are horticulturists; they cannot distinguish a pea from a carrot, or from anything else, for that matter. They do not care about their food's appearance.

4. The dog food's aroma and taste—aroma being the most important—are the critical factors to your dog. Be forewarned that what smells awful to you may smell wonderful to your dog. Some perfectly acceptable canned dog foods may actually cause you to gag when you open them, but if you can stand the odor and your Border Collie does well on the food, use the food.

Contents of the Dog Food

There is constant controversy today about the contents of dog foods, particularly canned dog foods. If you browse through pet journals or the Internet you will find printed or electronic sermons on every aspect of canine nutrition. Some of the pitches will be about "natural" diets for dogs, others will be excited about what goes into dog food, others will rattle on and on about all-meat diets. Some of these diatribes contain completely valid information and there is the catch—this core of truth can steer you away from perfectly good sources of canine nutrition.

The truth is, most premium commercial dog foods are more than adequate for your Border Collie's nutritional needs. You may have to pick and choose, but what your dog needs is already readily available. Working with your veterinarian, you should be able to find a premium-quality food that will fit your pet's needs.

Kibble Versus Canned Foods

The most commonly used forms of dog food are kibble and canned foods, in that order. Both have characteristics to recommend them. There are also things about kibbled and canned foods that argue against their use.

Kibbled foods: For our purposes, these will be defined as dog food made up primarily of vegetable products with added fat. Kibbled foods may also have added fish or animal

ulate you. If you have a picky dog and feel compelled to feed kibble for financial or other reasons, you may be able to strike a happy medium. Select a premium-quality kibble; if the dog will not eat the kibble, dress it up with a little canned food. The canned food will provide a more appealing taste for him; the kibble will provide texture—something for the dog to chew—and the combination will keep the cost reasonable.

Canned food: This is easily stored and all it takes to prepare it is a can opener, a feed bowl of some sort, and a dog that is agreeable to being fed. The single most important recommendation for canned food is that dogs find it more appealing than other forms of food.

The downside to canned food is that it is considerably more expensive than kibbled foods. The cost of feeding canned food can be prohibitive, especially if more than one dog is involved.

There is no need to go overboard with the canned food. A quarter of a can should be more than enough to tempt your Border Collie's taste buds.

Roll-your-own dog rations: There is a tendency in all of us to want to believe that by adding this or that we can make a perfect dog food. A few generations ago, anyone offering a commercial dog food would have been bankrupt shortly after beginning production. People fed dogs what they had left over from the table. Families were larger then; people ate more and had more leftovers. True, puppy mortality was probably higher, more dogs very likely suffered from problems that could have been

protein sources. Typically, kibble is sold in bags, although some kibble is sold in small boxes. Kibble is the food of choice for individuals with a large number of dogs. It is relatively less expensive than other types of dog food of similar quality. The most expensive kibble is still less expensive than canned foods offering the same ingredients and quality.

Because kibble is dry it is also easier to feed, less messy, and generally more pleasant to be around than most canned foods. Kibbled foods are also more easily measured when monitoring food intake. Some kibble is as nutritious as any other form of dog food, but there is a catch: No matter what the nutritional value of a dog food is, if it is not eaten, it does no good.

Some dogs absolutely will not eat kibble. A great deal of what a dog will eat is determined by his early diets and how much he can manip-

handled by a better diet, and a lot of dogs never reached their true potential.

In recent years, dog-feeding practices have been greatly changed by a general decline in family size. There has also been a shift of population from rural areas to cities and suburbs. The ready availability of relatively inexpensive commercial dog foods has had its impact on dog feeding. The vast majority of dog owners feed a premium kibbled or canned food. Certainly, the vast majority of professional breeders and trainers feed only a commercially prepared product appropriate to the breed, the activity of the dog, and his age. It is an excellent example to follow.

The single biggest problem with home cooking your dog food is getting everything in balance. Too much protein in a young dog's diet could lead to OCD as can too much calcium. Too much fat in the home-brewed feed can create overweight pets. It is especially difficult to get the right balance of vitamins and minerals. An unbalanced diet can cause growth difficulties, orthopedic problems, and other physical and mental problems too great to list.

If you are pondering going into the dog food business at home, answer the following questions:
• How is your Border Collie doing on his present diet?
• Have you spoken to your veterinarian about your pet's diet?
• Do you know what should be included in a dog food?
• Do you know where to get the ingredients you will need?
• Do you have the facilities you will need for making your creation?
• Can you afford the homemade dog food?
• Do you have a complete organic chemistry lab in your basement?

• Do you have the time to put into making the food?
• Can you actually make something better for your Border Collie than a commercial manufacturer, especially considering the varieties of food on the market?

If the answer to the first question is "OK," or "Great," then why bother making your own food. If the answer to the next question is, "No," you are definitely getting ahead of yourself. If the answers to the rest of the questions are "No," dig deeper into the available commercially produced dog foods for something that will suit your requirements and your pet's needs.

Note: You should consult your veterinarian before you do anything drastic. If you cannot get information you need locally, try your state school of veterinary medicine.

Dietary Requirements in Old Age

As dogs age they tend to become less active than when they were puppies. Old age in Border Collies may not arrive until age 12 or more. As they slow down, they may gain weight if their nutritional intake is not adjusted. Neutered dogs and older dogs may share this characteristic. Fats should certainly be reduced in the older Border Collie's diet; without the youthful activity, a high-fat diet can result in a high-fat Border Collie. The fats removed from the older dog's diet should be replaced with carbohydrates.

Commercial manufacturers produce a variety of products for older dogs. Depending upon your Border Collie's activity level, history of injuries, and age, you should be able to find a food suitable to its needs. Consult with your veterinarian before making drastic changes.

ACTIVITIES FOR YOUR BORDER COLLIE

One way to keep your Border Collie healthy and happy is to burn off some of his energy in a way that he will enjoy. Thanks to the breed's intelligence and flexibility there are any number of these outlets available.

Aside from having a surprisingly high level of intelligence, a relatively long body, long tail, and long legs, Border Collies are a highly variable breed. They vary in temperament from bold and aggressive to "soft," shy, and retiring. Size varies as much as temperament. There are very few absolutes relating to Border Collies, but the one thing that is absolute is this: Border Collies *must* have something to do. Those that are taken into homes that provide every other need except for a special activity may become neurotic, destructive, or unpredictable.

Before buying or accepting a Border Collie into your life, have plans to include some activity along with the dog.

Some Border Collies are always ready to play catch. This one even brought its own ball and glove.

Trialing

Over the last 30 years or so, the number of stockdog trials has increased dramatically. These trials bring out the best in the breed, as well as providing exercise for the dog and the handler. On just about any weekend during the spring, early summer, and fall, a stockdog trial is taking place within driving distance of your home. The trials are sanctioned, sponsored, or even put on by state, local, or national Border Collie associations. Rules for the trials are standardized around the trial rules put forward by the International Sheep Dog Society, although American courses tend to be somewhat shorter.

Requirements: Trialing is a hobby that requires three things: time, effort, and patience. A good dog helps, too. Dogs may be obtained already trained or they may be trained from scratch. Either way, trial dogs

Trial work requires that stock, usually sheep, be moved quickly and quietly over a course of gates, panels, and pens in order to emulate natural working conditions.

must be worked daily and trained constantly. It is axiomatic on the trial circuit that trials are won at home, not on the trial course. What this means, of course, is that the handler cannot expect more of the dog than the dog knows how to give. If the handlers allow sloppy work on a daily basis, they can expect exactly the same thing on the trial course.

Length of Courses: Trial courses in the United States will range from 300 to 440 yards (274–402 m), a few longer. In Great Britain, trial courses may run to 800 yards (732 m).

Sheep Trials: Sheep trials will require that the dog be sent out on command to gather the sheep. Ultimately, the dog and handler will be required to bring the sheep around the handler, drive them through two freestanding gates, and pen them. Most trials will require that one or more sheep be "shed" or cut out of the flock.

Levels: Except at Championship level trials, there will be more than one level at which to compete. Typically, these levels are arranged so as to allow for the skills of beginning handlers and/or the experience of young Border Collies.

The AKC Herding Program

The American Kennel Club sponsors a herding program for a number of herding breeds, including the Border Collie. The program is divided into two classifications: Testing and Trial.

Testing: The Test classification offers two titles: Herding Test Dog (HT) and Pre-Trial Tested Dog (PT). In order to qualify for the Herding Test Dog, the dog simply has to show some inherent ability to herd stock and some degree of trainability. The Pre-Trial Tested Dog has some training and can move stock over a simple course.

Trial classification: The Trial classification has four titles. Herding Started (HS), Herding Intermediate (HI), and Herding Excellent (HX)

This little girl, about 9 years old, is working an adult Border Collie on adult ewes with admirable confidence. With a little time, a Border Collie, some sheep, a little training for the trainer, and some patience, anyone can do it—but maybe not as well as this girl.

are the three progressively more difficult titles. After a Border Collie earns the HX, he can then work toward accumulating 15 Championship points and the Herding Championship (HCH).

Other Trials

Trials based on ISDS rules differ from American Kennel Club herding events in that they are purely competitions. Titles are given only to winners of specific events and then for only one year.

To be competitive at Border Collie trials, you will need

- a Border Collie from good stock
- a place to train your dog
- stock to use in training
- some training for yourself

Most of the better handlers and dogs at stockdog trials are farmers, ranchers, or people who work their dogs with stock every day. The best trial dogs are also the best everyday working dogs. If you intend to compete and intend to have the competition mean anything, plan to spend hours every day practicing and training your Border Collie. Trialing provides all the purpose and exercise of farm work along with the opportunity to meet and socialize with some truly fine people.

Obedience

Not only is Obedience a basic necessity for any dog, the trials offered through Obedience trials and competitions can occupy a Border Collie and his owner for years.

Obedience Training Levels

There are three levels of competition in basic Obedience: Novice, Open, and Utility. If these levels of competition are pursued, they can result in Companion Dog (CD), Companion Dog Excellent (CDX), and Utility Dog (UD) titles, respectively.

Exercises

There are six exercises in Novice class:
1. Heel on leash
2. Stand for examination
3. Heel off leash
4. Recall
5. Long sit
6. Long down

Open work includes
- Heel off leash
- Long sit
- Long down
- Down on recall
- Stand for examination
- Retrieve on the flat
- Retrieve over the high jump
- Broad jump

Utility level work includes
- Signal exercise
- Directed jumping
- Directed retrieve
- Two scent discrimination tests

Scores

The American Kennel Club scores all Obedience competitions levels the same. A perfect score in Novice, Open, and Utility competitions is 200. In order to earn any of the Obedience titles, a competitor must earn a minimum of 170 points in three competitions. Successful completion of a competition is referred to as "earning a leg." Even with a score of 170 or more points, earning a leg requires that at least 50 percent of possible points must be scored on all exercises. A competitor cannot specialize in recall or drop on command and completely blow the heeling exercises; a dog competing in Obedience must be competent in all exercises if he is to get a "leg." With three legs, a Novice dog earns his Companion Dog certificate, an open competitor earns a Companion Dog Excellent certificate, and a contestant in the Utility class will pick up his Utility Dog diploma.

After earning the Utility Dog (UD) certificate, Obedience competitors can attempt to earn points toward an Obedience Trial Championship (OTCH). Competitors can earn these points by placing first or second in an Open B or Utility Class. If the Utility Class is divided, only Utility B qualifies. In order to become an Obedience Trial Champion, a competitor must win 100 points in competition to include

✔ A first place in Utility (Utility B, if divided) with three dogs competing.

✔ A first place in Open B with at least six dogs in competition.

✔ Another first in either of the two classes mentioned above, under the same conditions.

The three firsts must be earned under three different judges.

Where to Get Obedience Training for Your Border Collie

If you do not know someone who can recommend a good Obedience trainer, there are several alternative sources of information. First, try contacting the kennel club in your area. If you cannot find the local kennel club in your yellow pages, wait for a while—kennel clubs advertise bench and Obedience events long before they occur. By reading your local newspaper you should have ample notification of upcoming Obedience trials. Most advertisements will include a number for registration that you can

A young Border Collie meeting a Golden Retriever in Obedience class demonstrates why Obedience training is important.

call to ask for a list of Obedience trainers. If the local club keeps such information, they are typically more than eager to pass on such lists. As a rule, though, clubs will not provide recommendations.

If you can get a list, pick someone close to where you live and visit one or two of the classes. If you like the trainer and the trainer's methods, sign up for the next class. If the trainer turns out to be unacceptable, find the next-closest class and spend some time watching that trainer. It should not take more than a class or two before you find a trainer who suits your needs.

If you cannot come up with any leads locally, try calling or writing to the American Kennel Club. They will have a list of all Obedience trials in your area as well as clubs and organizations that might be able to help you.

course, one that has at least one jump, as well as showing higher-level cooperation between the Border Collie and the handler.

Rules for Rally-O can be found at: *www.akc.org/pdfs/rulebooks/RO2999.pdf.*

Signs used at Rally-O can be found at: *www.akc.org/pdfs/rulebooks/ROR999.pdf.*

Rally-O

Rally-O is the newest show event from the AKC. It is an odd mixture of Obedience, Agility, and speed. There are three levels of competition, Novice, Advanced, and Excellent. There are 12 to 20 stations on the courses, depending on the level of participation. All stations have signs that instruct the handler what to do.

All Novice activities are performed on leash. The tasks include *sit, down, stay, come,* and knowledge of the *heel* position. Advanced is a set of a similar set of activities performed off leash and including at least one jump. Excellent requires that the dog run a much more difficult

Frisbee

Chasing and catching a Frisbee is something that comes easily to many Border Collies. Calm, confident Border Collies will see the disk in the air and become intrigued by this new mystery; others will be indifferent and, unless they are actually struck with the Frisbee, they will pretty much ignore it. Disinterested dogs will sit and watch you throw the Frisbee until your arm is numb, while some will take the fact that you have thrown a Frisbee in their direction as a reprimand. They will slink off or run away from you and the disk. If this happens, consider another activity.

Frisbee is another excellent way of burning off some of your Border Collie's excess energy, providing that it is the least bit interested in catching it.

lies can be exercised in a relatively limited area with a Frisbee. It requires only a park or small field to throw the disk. If your dog is adept enough, there are local and national competitions, and if Fleet is especially good, one of the national dog food companies sponsors a team of Border Collies that tours and puts on Frisbee demonstrations. Your dog might just qualify for professional status!

A note of caution: Border Collies are extremely athletic and highly competitive. If they are interested in catching the Frisbee, they will go to great lengths to come down with one thrown in their direction. High leaps and spins in the air are common in this sport. Problems may arise when a dog spins in the air, lands off balance, and injures himself. Care should be taken to throw the Frisbee so that it can be caught, and in such a way that the Border Collie can land safely. Young dogs should not have their physical abilities overtaxed. When starting out, keep the Frisbee close to the ground. Concentrate on distance rather than height with younger dogs. It is also important that you work with one of the softer Frisbees made especially for dogs in order to prevent a great deal of the tooth damage that can occur with Frisbees made for humans.

Technique

If your Border Collie will play "fetch," he has potential as a Frisbee dog. Instead of throwing a stick or ball for him to retrieve, throw a Frisbee. Throw it close to him after getting him excited, using the same words you use to get him excited about fetching a stick or ball. If the dog retrieves the Frisbee, or even walks over to where it has fallen, be lavish with your praise. Throw the Frisbee again, just a little farther than the first throw. If your Border Collie retrieves faster or improves his performance at all, praise him lavishly. Over time, he will learn that catching the Frisbee in the air is more exciting than retrieving it from the ground. With practice, he can execute all the moves you have seen performed on television.

Benefits

For the Border Collies that take to the Frisbee, it is an excellent form of exercise. It also has the benefit of being relatively inexpensive—maintenance and upkeep on Frisbees are much less costly than on sheep or cattle. Border Col-

Flyball

Flyball, a bizarre sport invented in California in the 1970s, has very little to do with anything except a good time. The actual competition of flyball requires at least two teams of four dogs each. There is a course, 51 feet (15.5 m) in length. The first of four hurdles is 6 feet (1.8 m) from the starting line. Hurdles are spaced 10 feet (3 m) apart. Fifteen feet (4.6 m) past the last hurdle is a spring-loaded box.

Object

The object of the competition is for the first dog to go over the hurdles to the box. When the dog presses the top of the box, a tennis ball is shot upward. The dog is supposed to catch the ball and return to the finish line, over the hurdles. When the first dog crosses the finish line, the second dog can go. The first team to have all four members compete without errors wins.

Flyball is fun and does provide some exercise. It is a way for the owner and the Border Collie to spend time together. It will not provide all the exercise required for an adult Border Collie, however; some other form of exercise will have to be provided.

Like trialing, flyball may be pursued at any number of levels, from local fun competitions all the way to the national level. It, too, provides the opportunity to spend time with the dogs and with the people who love them.

Tracking

The activity of tracking is pretty much what the name implies: A dog is trained to follow a scent trail. The activity is a natural for all dogs. Their highly developed sense of smell makes olfactory input as important as any other sense. Even breeds not normally associated with tracking can do well.

The American Kennel Club offers three titles in the tracking category:

1. Dogs that successfully complete a basic test may have the title Tracking Dog (TD) placed after their name.

2. Completion of a more difficult and advanced test gives them the right to use Tracking Dog Excellent (TDX).

3. The Variable Surface Tracking Test (VST) is an even more difficult test over a number of different types of surfaces. The dog may be asked to follow a trail over grass, pavement, concrete, and/or dirt.

Once a dog has earned his TD, TDX, and VST, he may have the title Champion Tracker (CT).

Agility

Agility began as something to fill breaks during horse-jumping competitions. Agility competition is a timed event over a course that looks remarkably like a miniature horse-jumping course with some additional obstacles added.

The walk rail doesn't slow down this Border Collie in an Agility competition.

Here, a tricolor Border Collie clears a hurdle with room to spare.

Dogs will be asked to go over hurdles, climb ramps, crawl through pipes, walk along rails, and run through "weave poles," a slalom-like arrangement of poles. The competitors are required to run the course in a prescribed order, with a given starting and ending point. The dog

A young Border Collie is not at all challenged by the ramp.

that completes the course with the lowest time and the fewest faults wins. Faults are awarded by judges for not taking an obstacle cleanly.

Every Agility trial is potentially different from every other trial. Even second and third runs may differ in the course layout and/or the order of the obstacles. Obviously, the critical aspects of Agility training are training and communication between dog and handler. As an extra incentive, Border Collies that are registered with the American Kennel Club can compete for titles in Agility, earning the following titles: Novice Agility (NA), Open Agility (OA), Agility Excellent (AX), and Master Agility Excellent (MX).

Border Collies do exceptionally well in Agility competitions due to their natural athleticism, intelligence, and trainability.

Scent Hurdles

This is another strange sport. Basically a variation on flyball, it uses the same course size, the same hurdles and rules for hurdles. The difference is that there are four balls, one of which has been scented by the dog's trainer. The idea is for the dog to get over the hurdles, select the correct ball, and return to the finish line. Scent hurdles add an interesting twist to an already fun activity.

Like Flyball, this is an enjoyable activity at which Border Collies can excel. Unfortunately, scent hurdles will not provide enough exercise for the normal, healthy Border Collie and should be augmented with more strenuous exercise.

Show Events

Because this section is about activities that will provide exercise for Border Collies, very little will be said about show events. For information concerning physical standards and bench trials, contact the Border Collie Club of America (BCCA) and/or the American Kennel Club (AKC). Postal and E-mail addresses will be provided in the references (page 92).

Water Activities

As a group, Border Collies love the water. If one is fortunate enough to have access to water, he will probably spend a great deal of his time swimming. Swimming is an ideal recreation for Border Collies in warmer areas or during the warm months of the year. Your Border Collie can exercise as much as he needs to without fear of heat exhaustion or heatstroke. A family with children will appreciate the Border Collie's love of water; however, care should be taken when a Border Collie spends a great deal of time in, or around, water. His dense

Border Collies are not water dogs, but most of them do seem to enjoy life around the water. With proper care they can enjoy life at a river, lake, or quiet beach.

undercoat holds water close to the skin and in hot, damp areas, the Border Collie can develop fungus infections and other skin diseases.

Skin problems: If you live in such an area, be sure that you monitor your Border Collie's skin condition. At the first sign of fungus or, "hot spots," get him to a veterinarian for treatment. It may be necessary to limit your dog's access to water in order to minimize skin problems. Border Collies that have ready access to water may also develop ear problems.

Sledding

In colder areas of the country, Border Collies have been used in sled teams. Admittedly, they were not bred to pull loads, but their intelligence and energy has made them valuable members of dog teams, especially as lead dogs.

TRAINING

Because they are so energetic and enthusiastic, the Border Collie requires as much or more socialization training as any other breed. Fortunately, the ancestors of Border Collies have been bred for intelligence and ease of training.

Basic Training for Your Border Collie

With the possible exception of fingernails on a chalkboard, there are few things in life more irritating than an out-of-control dog. Most out-of-control dogs get that way from lack of training and discipline. Well-trained dogs, no matter what breed, are typically a pleasure to be around. Border Collie owners and trainers do have a certain advantage over other dog owners since their dogs are easier to train, but of course, untrained Border Collies are no more pleasant to be around than any other breed. Not only will some minimum level of training make your Border Collie more pleasant to be with, it could literally save his life.

One Border Collie owner tells the story of his first Border Collie. The dog was only three or four months old but the owner had already

This white-faced Border Collie demonstrates the variety of the breed's markings.

taught him to *down, come,* and *stay.* The puppy was raised as a housedog and had little experience outside his own backyard. One afternoon, while the Border Collie's owner was away from home, the owner's wife answered the front doorbell. The puppy, excited by the presence of a stranger, ran out the door and toward a busy street. With no other options, the wife yelled, "*Down!*" as loudly as she could. The runaway puppy dropped as if he had been shot, about 6 inches (15 cm) from the pavement. Not only had training put the puppy under control, it had probably saved his life.

Various Approaches to Training

In the course of trying to train your Border Collie, you will come across as many different training styles as there are trainers. You will be presented with raw behavior modification where every desired behavior is rewarded or

Training Approaches

All training approaches have one thing in common: They view the Border Collie's entire life as a training session. Every time a dog is worked, every time it is run through its paces, it is in a learning situation. If it is allowed to be sloppy in accepting commands, it will become sloppy. If it is held close to its commands, it will work as it has been trained. Moreover, every time a Border Collie is worked, the handler can zero in on problems and weaknesses that the dog may have.

"reinforced" and every undesirable behavior is punished. Other approaches take advantage of the "alpha male" behavior inherent in all dogs.

It is very easy to become distracted by the variety of techniques and philosophies in use. If you are inexperienced at training dogs, your best bet is to locate as many amateur and professional trainers as you can find and pick their brains. You will probably be surprised at how willing dog people are to talk about how they do things. You may even want to sit in on a few basic Obedience classes. After all this you will certainly find a training technique, or a set of training techniques, that will suit you best. There are all manner of trainers using a wide variety of training methods with a great deal of success. The only commonalities you will find will be consistency, willingness to perform the same training procedures over and over, and the use of correction rather than punishment.

Pick and choose among the techniques until you get the results you want. The truth is, it does not matter what training technique you use as long as it works.

The techniques presented in this chapter are not based on any belief that they are the only way to approach that type of training, but because they have been proven to work.

Basic Commands

1. Try to make the training sessions fun.

2. Encourage your pet and use praise freely.

3. The training collar should be used only to keep the dog's head up in the early stages of training.

4. Do not forget that he is young and inexperienced. If you lose your temper and jerk the young dog around, he may sour on training all together.

5. Finally, keep the sessions brief. A 15-minute training period is more than enough in the beginning.

Sit

You will not actually be teaching your Border Collie to sit; except in extreme cases of hip dysplasia, Border Collies sit as a normal part of their behavior. It will be your job to teach him when and where to sit.

Before you begin training, put the training collar on your Border Collie correctly. Attach the training lead to the free end of the collar, making certain that the collar will move freely.

There are several approaches to teaching a dog to sit:

✔ Probably the easiest method is to position your dog on your left, take up the slack in your lead, and say, "*Fleet, sit.*"

Punishment

No dog should ever be called to its handler to be punished. Even mild correction should not be given if the Border Collie has just obeyed a *come* command. Border Collies are exceptionally bright. Not only can they learn to come quickly; they can learn *not* to come if something unpleasant is done to them after they obey. Nothing is more frustrating than calling a Border Collie and having him sit 8 or 10 yards (7–9 m) from you and watch while you call.

✔ A moment later, push the dog's rear downward. Keep his head up with the leash to prevent his first *sit* attempts from becoming *downs*.

✔ Always say the dog's name, followed about a second later by the *sit* command. Your voice should be loud and firm enough to be heard, but yelling is not required.

The first attempts at getting a *sit* out of your Border Collie will probably not be all that elegant. If he is particularly shy, he may try to back up or fight the leash. Give him time to recover and get used to the idea that you are not going to strangle him or crush his pelvis.

If you have even the approximation of a *sit*, lavish the dog with praise. Do not get so carried away that you scare him, but let him know you approve.

If your dog resists the downward push on his rear, try putting pressure on the back of his "knees." If he sits or half-sits, then praise and pet him.

A handler teaching a Border Collie to **sit.**

Allow your Border Collie to get back to his feet and start all over. Keeping his head up, say "*Fleet, sit,*" and push his rear down. You should expect the *sit* to be better and more complete this time. If he actually sits or comes closer to sitting, praise him again. With repetition and consistency, your Border Collie will begin to sit when he hears, "*Sit.*"

Stay

Your Border Collie will have to have a good handle on the *sit* command before you can teach him to *stay*.

Teaching an active puppy to sit, and eventually to stay, will make life easier for the handler and the puppy.

✔ Start the training exercise by sitting your Border Collie next to your left leg. When he is settled, say, "*Stay,*" and move a step away from him.

✔ At the same time you take your step, put your hand in front of his face. If he moves, put him back in position.

✔ Let him sit for a second or two, then say "*OK*" and allow him to come to you.

✔ If he has done well, praise him; make it clear that you are pleased with what he has done.

✔ In the early stages the young Border Collie will probably not understand why you are so pleased. He will understand only that you are pleased and will work to continue pleasing you.

✔ As you repeat the training steps above, gradually increase the distance that you move from your Border Collie and the time he *stays.*

✔ The *stay* is as demanding of consistency as any of the commands in Obedience training.

You will have to watch the young dog closely after issuing the *stay* command. If he fidgets or leans, he will likely stand and you will have to move quickly to keep him seated.

✔ Put your hand in front of his face and say, "*Stay*" again. Eventually, you will be able to move well away from your dog and leave him sitting for a considerable time.

Remember that your dog is new to the *stay* command. A high-energy dog such as the Border Collie does not naturally stay in one place for very long. Before he can learn to stay, he must successfully stay for a few seconds.

Note: Do not get impatient and punish your dog—that can only lead to confusion and the necessity of retraining. Keep things light and the sessions short, especially at the beginning.

Come

After your dog has learned the *sit* and *stay,* he is ready to master the *come* command. Your Border Collie has very likely been coming to you since he arrived, but now you need to teach him that "*Come*" is a command and not a whim.

✔ Give your pet the *sit* command followed by the *stay* command.

✔ Walk to the end of the training lead and turn to face your dog.

✔ Put all the enthusiasm you can into your voice and say, "*Fleet, come.*"

✔ If the dog does not come immediately, give a gentle tug on the training lead. If he still does not come, tug a little harder.

✔ When your dog comes to you, praise and pet him. Let him know that you are pleased.

✔ After you have rewarded your Border Collie with praise, let him calm down for a few minutes. Give the *sit/stay* command again.

✔ Move to the end of the leash, face your dog, and say, "*Fleet, come*" in an excited voice.

✔ Again, use the lead to encourage the dog to come if he is hesitant.

✔ Be extravagant with praise when your dog does what you want him to.

The lead: When you have your Border Collie coming dependably within the length of the training lead, place him on a longer lead. There are a number of commercially made leads for use in training. You can also make a perfectly good dragline from a piece of soft nylon rope 20 feet (6.1m) long with a chrome snap on one end and a large knot at the other. This lead can be used to gradually increase the distance between you and your Border Collie until the entire 20 feet (6.1m) is used. At that point you can begin to work off lead.

Come may be the most critical of the commands in the set discussed here. A dog that will come instantly on command is a convenience to the handler/trainer.

Heel

The *heel* command is also handy. It makes moving around in crowds with your dog easy, even pleasant. The idea of the *heel* command is to teach your Border Collie to stay on your left, starting and stopping when you do.

✔ Begin by giving the *sit/stay* command. The dog should be positioned to your left as in the beginning stages of the *sit* command.

✔ Take up the slack in the lead, putting light upward pressure on the training collar. Hold the lead in your right hand as you step forward off your left foot.

✔ As you make your first step, say, "*Fleet, heel.*" If Fleet does not step out with you, urge him forward with a gentle tug on the

A young Border Collie being taught to come.

training collar. If he hesitates, get his attention by popping the loose end of the lead against your leg.

✔ Repeat the command, name and all, as you walk forward. If he moves with you, praise him.

✔ Keep moving with the puppy's shoulders just even with your legs. If he moves ahead or lags behind, correct him with light pressure on his collar. If he gets completely out of line, stop what you are doing, give the *sit/stay* command, and start over.

✔ If Fleet moves well with you, continue praising him as you walk. When you stop, give the *sit* command. Ultimately, he will learn that he should sit when you stop and walk at heel when you step off on the left foot.

Your pet should focus his attention on you as you walk. Getting the undivided attention of an energetic young Border Collie may take some work—the younger the Border Collie, the more work it will take.

A trainer demonstrating heel on leash. In more advanced work, the Border Collie will be taught to heel off leash, a very handy command.

Direction: Some handlers will make sudden changes in direction in order to keep their dog's attention on them. Others recommend that the trainer carry a piece of raw liver in his or her mouth while working the dog. Not surprisingly, the direction change method has met with greater popularity than the liver technique.

Without a leash: If you keep at it, your Border Collie will heel without a leash. Working off lead is especially handy if you have an armful

of packages. If you move around in crowded areas or plan to compete in Obedience trials, the *heel* command is critical.

Down

The *down* command is particularly useful for Border Collies that will later be trained for stock work—in fact, the *down* command is a prerequisite for stock work. It is also vital for anyone who takes a Border Collie out around other people.

✔ Start *down* training with your Border Collie to your left, just as you did when beginning *sit* training.

✔ The training collar should be on your dog correctly and the training lead attached.

✔ Give your dog the *sit/stay* command; say, "*Sam, down.*" Use the lead to pull his head down.

Anxiety: Some Border Collies will be frightened at being pulled down. If your dog shows signs of anxiety, stop what you are doing until he calms down. Give the *sit/stay* command again and use the chain to pull his head down again. If any progress is made toward an elbow down, stomach on the ground position, praise and pet your dog. After praising Sam and allowing him time to calm down, return him to the *sit/stay* position. Repeat the *down* command using your dog's name. Again, pull downward on the training lead. If your dog moves toward the *down* position, lavish him with praise. If you take your time and remain patient, your Border Collie will lose his fear of being downed.

Some Border Collies are stubborn about being downed. Large males may be particularly difficult. With these animals you may have to take a different tack.

This trainer is using hand signals to down her Border Collie. Voice commands work just as well.

✔ Position your dog to your left and give the *sit/stay* command. Repeat "*Sam, down.*" Pull downward on the training lead.

✔ If he refuses to move downward, grasp both of his front legs just below the knee, gently fold his legs, and position him on the ground.

✔ Praise him extravagantly.

✔ Let him calm down for a few minutes before you start over.

✔ It will not take long for your Border Collie to learn that *down* means he should take a position with elbows and stomach on the ground. This method also works well with shy dogs.

Down/stay: After your dog has mastered the *down*, you can begin work on the *down/stay* combination. Training for this combination is identical to the *sit/stay* command combination, except the *down* precedes the *stay*.

The *down* command is especially helpful in controlling excitable young Border Collies. A Border Collie in the *down* position has to do more shifting and bunching in order to get out of a *down* position than one in a sitting position. A perceptive trainer can catch a puppy before he can break his *down*. With patience and time, a Border Collie can be downed and left for extended periods.

House-training

The easiest way to house-train a puppy is simply to never give him the opportunity to defecate or urinate in the house. Your job as the trainer is to make it easy for the puppy to go outside regularly and often. Try to schedule the puppy's arrival at your home at the beginning of a long weekend or a vacation when someone will be around the puppy at all times. Do not bring a new puppy into your home when you expect a lot of visitors. Christmas, Thanksgiving, and other family holidays will generally have too much commotion in your home for the puppy to be introduced successfully.

Tricks to Help

There are a couple of tricks you might use to make house-training a little easier.

✔ Take an old towel to the breeder's and have them put it in with the puppies; then retrieve the blanket and place it in your new Border Collie's crate. The odor of the litter and the puppy's mother will help identify the crate as being home. This will not only help prevent the puppy from fouling the crate, it will make the transition from breeder to your home easier.

TIP

Training a Dog

In any situation, only one member of a group can be dominant. In the example of a human training a dog, it is very easy for the the dog to take charge. To avoid this, all training should be reasonable, all commands should be enforced if ignored, and the handler should remember that commands are not suggestions.

✔ The other, and less pleasant, thing you can do is to sack up some droppings or straw upon which the puppy or his siblings have relieved themselves.

✔ Put this scented "bait" in an area where you would prefer the puppy to do his business. By "salting the mine" in this manner, you have created a spot the puppy automatically associates with his natural functions.

✔ The day you bring the puppy home, stop by this preselected spot and let him relieve himself before you take him into the house. Do not just

put him down and expect him to go as if he were on command.

✔ Give him a few minutes to do the normal sniffing and site selection that all dogs do. Be prepared to wait a while for the puppy to find the perfect spot.

✔ After he has voided, the chance of his fouling your house is reduced and the site is further marked as an acceptable spot for such activities.

✔ When you finally take the new puppy inside, make sure that there will be someone available to monitor his activities at all times. At the first sign of restlessness or whimpering, take him out to his spot and wait—better yet, have regularly scheduled trips outside.

✔ One trip should be the first thing in the morning; others should be planned for after meals. There should always be an extended trip before you and your family go to bed. Remember, there can never be too many trips for a young puppy.

Accidents

You should understand that there will probably be accidents. No matter how fast the puppy progresses, changes in food or the onset of sickness can cause the puppy to foul your carpet or floor. If this happens, do not waste your time scolding the puppy. Clean the floor with deodorizing cleanser and let it dry before you let the puppy back into the area. By deodorizing the area, you will prevent him from making the association with your carpet and bowel movements.

Let your puppy find a place, within limits, that it selects for bowel movements and urination. The area can be influenced by depositing some of his droppings in an acceptable area.

By creating an area outside the house, this owner is obviously trying to teach the Border Collie the difference between inside and outside as far as house-training goes.

Note: Punishment should never be used in house-training. The practice of rubbing a puppy's nose in his mistakes is a definite waste of time—all you will have after a few such episodes is a smelly puppy that avoids you.

Travel Training

There are a number of things you can do to make an automobile trip with your Border Collie safe and pleasant:

✔ Pack a survival kit containing first aid products and medications, including motion sickness medications.

✔ Never leave your dog alone in a closed car. Even in moderate weather the inside temperature of a closed car can rise to over 100°F (37.8°C), causing your dog to suffer heatstroke and death.

✔ Never allow your Border Collie to ride with his head out of the window. He will enjoy the wind in his face, but it is extremely dangerous. Think about the number of times your windshield has been scarred by gravel thrown up by the car in front of you and imagine the damage that same piece of gravel could cause to your pet's eyes. Small pieces of sand and insects can also cause damage to eyes and mucous membranes.

✔ Always keep your Border Collie in his crate while the automobile is in motion.

✔ If you plan to stay overnight in a motel or hotel, call ahead to find accommodations that welcome pets.

✔ Carry a supply of the food that your dog normally eats. Changing food can result in an upset stomach; the road is possibly the worst place in the world for a pet to have that problem.

✔ Schedule your trip so you can stop every hour to exercise your dog. Rest areas along interstate highways usually provide exercise and comfort areas for dogs. Campgrounds and some truck stops provide similar facilities.

✔ Keep your Border Collie on a leash when he is out of the crate. Rest areas and motel parking lots may have puddles of antifreeze, screws, broken glass, and other items that are dangerous to your Border Collie.

✔ Keep your Border Collie in the crate in the motel or hotel room.

✔ Have your dog up to date on all inoculations. If you plan to cross international boundaries, have a valid health certificate with you.

✔ Pack your Border Collie's chew toys, favorite towel or blanket, and anything else that might make him feel at home.

HOW-TO: CRATE TRAINING

One of the first purchases you should make if you intend to keep your Border Collie in the home is a wire crate, or well-built plastic carrier. Crate-train him using the steps discussed below. Later, when it is necessary to take the puppy to the veterinarian or to travel with him, the crate will be familiar and comforting. Also, when it is necessary to confine the young dog for any length of time, there will be no problem getting him into the crate.

• Take your Border Collie out for an extended period before shutting him up for the night. Be sure that he has eliminated before you bring him back inside. Do not be in a hurry.

• Place the crate in a spot where the puppy can see family activities but where there is some peace and quiet. The crate should be in a spot that does not get blasted by cold drafts when a door is opened, and should not be directly in front of a heating vent or in direct sunlight during the summer. Find a place where you would be comfortable and put the crate there.

• Buy a crate that your puppy can grow into. Do not buy a puppy-sized crate that will have to be replaced as he grows.

• Buy the best crate or wire kennel you can afford. If necessary, you can partition the crate into sections using lightweight plywood. Parti-

tioning the crate will prevent the puppy from dividing it for his own purposes—sleep on one side, relief on the other.

• Before you put a young dog in the crate for the night, do what you can to burn up his excess energy. If you have children, let them play with the puppy but make sure they understand that roughhousing is not allowed—the object is to tire the puppy, not harm it.

• When the puppy is free in the house, leave the door of the crate open. This will allow the puppy to return to the crate for a nap or just to rest. Over time, the puppy will come to associate the crate with safety and quiet.

• If you have more than one dog, be sure to have enough crates to go around. Do not try to get by with fewer crates than you have dogs.

• Make certain that your puppy has something to entertain himself while he is awake. Keep one of his toys and a chewy in the crate but do not put so much in the crate that he has no room to stretch out.

• Do not feed or water your puppy in the crate. He needs to understand that he will be fed in the same place all the time, and that the crate is *not* that place.

All dogs should be crate trained, for their own comfort and as a step toward travel training.

• If the puppy is very young—six to nine weeks—put him in the crate, and schedule checks every two or three hours to see if he needs to go outside.

• If you are concerned that a puppy that you are to buy from a breeder will not adjust well at first, take steps to make his transition easier. Take something, an old cloth, even the bed the puppy is to sleep on, to the breeder. Have the breeder put the cloth or the bed into the area where the puppy's litter is being raised. After a day or two, the bed or cloth will acquire the comforting odor of the puppy's litter and mother. When the object is placed in the crate, the puppy will smell the odors he is used to and may actually seek out the crate.

• There will be puppies that have more difficulty than most adjusting to indoor life. If the addition of the mother and sibling-scented cloth or bed does not stop nighttime whimpering and crying, try adding a little warmth. Available on the Internet or at pet stores are any number of types of heating pads for dogs. If time is short, and no pet stores are available, try heating a brick until it is uncomfortably warm. Wrap it well in an old, heavy towel and seal the ends of the towel with duct tape. Place the heated brick inside the crate with the smell-impregnated bedding or cloth.

• If an older dog or a particularly aggressive cat is already living in the house when a young puppy arrives, the crate may not only feel like a place of safety, it may have to be used as one. If the older dog shows signs of jealousy, and becomes aggressive, the young dog may be in real danger. An aggressive cat may not be as dangerous, but will cause pain and fear through surprise. If you see an older dog or cat becoming aggressive toward the puppy, correct it

The safest way to transport your Border Collie is in a crate. But, no dog should ever be locked up in a closed vehicle, no matter what the temperature is. Cars are nothing more than rolling greenhouses.

immediately. Put the puppy in his crate, and put the older dog or cat outside. If the puppy learns to run to the crate and an older resident tries to get into the crate with it, you will have to correct the problem immediately no matter what it takes.

• If the puppy makes noise after being confined, try to quiet him by speaking sternly.

Punishment

Physical punishment will not work. In order to punish the puppy you will have to take him out of the crate and he will therefore be rewarded for making noise. By the time you get the puppy out of the crate, he will be confused about his punishment: Is he being punished for the noise he was making, the noise the crate made when the door opened, or the noise you may have made?

Schedule

Get up in the morning at your normal time. Do not change your schedule for the puppy.

HEALTH

7

Like all canines, Border Collies are subject to contagious diseases such as rabies, distemper, and hepatitis. But, like most modern breeds of dogs, they have acquired genetic problems through, "linebreeding," that is, closely breeding sires to daughters and granddaughters. It does make for better working Border Collies, but recessive genetic disorders can be a problem.

Hip Dysplasia

Hip dysplasia is a failure of the ball socket in the hip to develop as it should. Cartilage and natural fluids make a smooth, well-cushioned joint within the socket. In a normal dog, the ball joint of the leg is fully encased by the socket of the hip, but in a dysplastic dog the socket does not cover the ball joint completely. Cartilage and other lubricants may also be absent. In extreme cases, the ball joint is held against the pelvis only through the tension of the dog's leg and hip muscles.

Recent studies have shown that fat puppies have a much higher probability of developing canine hip dysplasia (CHD) than well-fed puppies weighing less. In some cases, litters have been divided in half, one group fed

Border Collies are generally a healthy breed, but there are special issues that must be considered.

according to instructions on the bag or can, the other about 25 percent less. It was not uncommon for the overfed puppies to all show CHD, while the food-controlled puppies were all dysplasia free. For more information, go to: *http://www.bordercollie.org/hd.html.*

Genes

Genes are the most reliable predictor of CHD. CHD is polygenic—the genes involved are numerous. Because of the complexity of the gene interactions in CHD, there may be varying degrees of severity in puppies from the same litter. Some may evidence no dysplasia while others may be so severely crippled that they must be euthanized.

Signs: Puppies may show signs of hip dysplasia as early as three to four months of age. As the puppy grows, he may not be as active as a normal puppy. There may also be a reluctance to climb onto and off raised surfaces. The owner may also notice a dysplastic puppy sitting with his pelvis leaning noticeably to one side. Some dogs may also "wobble" while walking, especially if tired. Owners should also be concerned if the chest and front legs of the animal are obviously much better developed than the hips. In extreme cases, the affected dog may yelp or whine when required to move.

Certification: Othopedic Foundation for Animals (OFA), PennHIP, and Cornell University offer certification of hips. While all of the behaviors listed above should be cause for concern, only a complete orthopedic and radiographic examination can accurately diagnose hip dysplasia. The Orthopedic Foundation for Animals (OFA), PennHIP, and more recently, Cornell, certify hips at levels unique to their organizations. It is especially important when selecting a puppy that OFA, PennHIP, or Cornell certifies both of his parents. Puppies should be certified by OFA, PennHIP, or Cornell by as soon as the organizational standards will allow.

Treatment: In moderate cases of hip dysplasia, treatment may be as simple as administering a couple of buffered aspirin a day. Some dysplastic dogs may benefit from surgery. Triple pelvic osteotomy is a type of surgery in which the pelvis is cut and repositioned to force a better fit between the femur and hip socket. More extreme cases may require complete hip replacement. Since hip surgery is expensive, it may not be an option for all dysplastic dogs. Consult your veterinarian before you undertake any treatment. In a small portion of diagnosed hip dysplasia cases, the Border Collie must be euthanized.

Prevention: The only effective method of preventing hip dysplasia is simply not breeding Border Collies that carry the complex genes for the disorder. All dogs found to be dysplastic should be neutered immediately. No matter how much your dog means to you, breeding gene-defective animals does not improve the breed. There are many excellent Border Collies available, most of them without defective genes. Again, buy and breed only OFA-certified stock.

Osteochondritis Desicans (OCD)

OCD is a defect or damage to the cartilage overlying the bones in a joint. Bone damage may also be present, to the extent that slivers of bone may show up in X-rays. Signs of lameness may appear in puppies around four months of age, gradually increasing in severity until the animal is severely limited in its movements at 12 months old.

Causes: Suggested causes of this problem include greater than normal activity, leaping off couches or steps, a genetic predisposition to cartilage damage, a diet too rich in protein and other nutrients, and calcium supplements.

Treatment: Treatment may be as simple as confining the puppy to limited movement or as extreme as surgery to remove damaged cartilage. Some veterinarians have had success combining confinement with a diet limited in protein.

Prevention: How do owners avoid OCD in their Border Collies? Suggestions include limiting activity until the puppy is a year or more in age and feeding a puppy food that contains reasonable levels of protein, fat, and other nutrients. A discussion of puppy nutrition with your veterinarian could help decide the specific brand of puppy food you select. As to limiting the activity of a Border Collie puppy—good luck!

A young tricolor Border Collie perks up for the camera.

Collie Eye Anomaly (CEA)

Border Collies, along with Standard Collies, Bearded Collies, and Shetland Sheepdogs, share the Collie Eye Anomaly. It is the most common source of genetic blindness in the Border Collie. In recent years it has increased in frequency along with the increased popularity of the breed. As with PRA, all Border Collie puppies should be tested for CEA. If you are considering a puppy, make sure that all puppies in the litter are certified as normal. Because the genetic dynamics of CEA are so complex, it is easier to avoid it than control it. Again, good Border Collies are being bred every day; if you cannot find a completely CEA-free litter, look a little harder. CEA is a genetic disease; there is now a DNA test for it. Have puppies tested by a veterinary ophthalmologist by 12 weeks of age to prove them clear of CEA. At the very least, have the parents tested genetically to make sure that at least one of them is free of Collie Eye Anomaly. If only one parent has CEA, the puppy can be only a carrier, not a victim. Typically, CEA does not result in blindness except in extreme cases but even Border Collies with mild CEA should never be bred.

Seizures

Seizures result from the prolonged firing of the neurons in the brain. Causes include injury to the brain, response to toxic substances, and heredity. Sometimes there is no obvious cause. These cases are referred to as "idiopathic," which, in this instance, means "I don't know where it comes from." In Border Collies the severity of the problem may vary greatly. Some Border Collies may simply appear to freeze in place or to ignore their owners briefly. Others may stagger and shake slightly. The most severe

Injured puppies like this one frequently become quieter and more dependent.

instances involve classic *grand mal* seizures in which the animal will fall to the ground and go into convulsions. Frequently, the dog may lose bladder and/or bowel control, may foam at the mouth, and, rarely, chew its own tongue.

Where seizures occur: If your Border Collie has seizures, perhaps the greatest danger arises from where the seizures occur. A Border Collie having seizures in the middle of a road is obviously in more danger than a Border Collie that has seizures in the kennel. Even *petit mal* seizures may cause your pet to fall off the top of his doghouse or down the steps. Border Collies that live around water and are prone to seizures risk falling into the water and drowning before they recover.

Effect: Usually, even severe seizures have little effect on the dog. Shortly after falling to the ground and convulsing, the victim of the seizures may be back on his feet, ready to play or work. However, when seizures come in series, or do not end quickly, there may be damage to the dog.

Treatment: Treatment for Border Collies with epilepsy (seizure disorder) is similar to the treatment for humans. Chemical treatments include primadone, phenobarbital, Valium, Dilantin, and others. Potassium bromide or sodium bromide, used in conjunction with phenobarbital or primadone, has proven highly effective in reducing seizures, but potassium bromide and sodium bromide are not commercially available to veterinarians. Both bromides must be bought as reagent grade chemicals and mixed with water by the veterinarian.

There are other problems with using bromide treatments including relatively high toxicity. As of this writing, neither potassium bromide nor sodium bromide was on the Food and Drug Administration's (FDA) list of drugs approved for use with canine seizures.

All chemical treatments could have toxic side effects to the point of damage to the liver or kidneys. Your veterinarian or a competent veterinary neurologist will typically be glad to talk to you about potential problems with drug treatment. Of course, when toxic substances or allergens bring on the seizures, the logical approach is to remove the problem substance from the dog's environment.

Prevention: Ask the breeder of any dog you are considering if there are seizures in the bloodline. If the breeder will not talk to you about the history of seizures, there are other breeders.

Contagious Diseases

Following is a discussion of various contagious diseases for which vaccinations are available.

Rabies

Rabies is the most widely known disease of dogs. Of course, rabies does not discriminate and will attack all mammals. It is typically transmitted to healthy animals through the bite of an infected animal. There is some reason to believe that the virus that causes rabies can also be transmitted through the mucous membranes or through breaks in the skin.

After infection, there is an incubation period of from three weeks to 120 days; the average incubation time is four to six weeks. Two days after the end of the incubation period, the infected animal will either go into the "furious" or "dumb" state.

The "furious" state: The "furious" state is the excited state most associated with rabies. While in this stage, the animal becomes irritable and snaps at anything he encounters, thereby transmitting the disease again. During this stage the animal will begin to have difficulty swallowing. Large amounts of saliva accumulate in the mouth. Since the animal cannot swallow, the saliva flows out of the mouth causing the characteristic "foaming at the mouth" of rabies. Though the rabid dog may be thirsty, he cannot drink. The dog may gag or cough, sometimes giving the impression that he has something stuck in his throat. Humans may be exposed to the virus at this point while trying to remove this nonexistent object. Within three to five days the infected animal will die of heart or respiratory failure.

Dumb rabies: "Dumb" rabies is simply rabies in which the excited stage is brief or skipped entirely. The animal dies just as surely and rapidly without the stereotypical behavior expected of rabid animals.

Prevention: Fortunately, rabies is easily avoided by inoculating puppies between the ages of three and five months and administering annual inoculations. Most states require rabies inoculations by law and provide low-cost inoculations at convenient sites. If you are not sold on rabies inoculations, remember that it is almost always fatal when contracted. Even worse, the only method of verifying exposure to rabies is by removing the brain from the skull and examining it. Discuss the vaccinations with your veterinarian. Remember, there is no cure.

Distemper

Aside from rabies, distemper has always been the disease most feared by dog owners. Like

Young Border Collies can be started on ducks or geese.

rabies, distemper is caused by a virus. Although it can occur in older dogs, distemper occurs most frequently in young dogs between the age of two months and one year. It typically begins with coldlike symptoms such as a runny nose, elevated fever, sneezing, watery eyes, and general lassitude. If the dog does not recover, the disease may progress to diarrhea, convulsions, neural damage, and paralysis. Even if the dog survives this stage, he is likely to have chorea, an uncontrollable twitching of the muscles. As distemper runs its course, the animal gradually becomes weaker and thinner. Death is common at this point.

If your Border Collie develops distemper or shows distemper-like symptoms, get him to the veterinarian as quickly as possible. Offer him as much liquid as he will drink and provide easily digested foods such as broth, egg yolks, and milk.

Prevention: Distemper is incurable, but it is preventable. Puppies should be vaccinated at 8 weeks, at 12 weeks, and again at 16 weeks. All dogs should receive annual boosters for distemper.

Like most of the diseases that afflict dogs, distemper is worse in underfed, or worm-infested, run-down dogs. After vaccination, keeping your Border Collie in good physical condition is the best method for preventing distemper.

Canine Parvovirus

When canine parvovirus (CPV) swept the United States in the late 1970s, whole kennels were decimated. Kennel owners would regularly lose every puppy, and sometimes, every dog in the kennel. Many Border Collie owners simply stayed home to avoid contact with the disease. There were stories of puppies that were healthy at breakfast and dead by dinner.

Parvoviruses are present in most mammals. They have been proven to cause fatal illnesses in cattle, pigs, and a number of other animals. In humans, parvoviruses cause problems ranging from childhood rashes, to eye and upper respiratory inflammation, and spontaneous abortions in women.

Parvo is frequently fatal in dogs, puppies especially. It affects the intestinal tract, the heart, or both. When parvo attacks the intestines, symptoms include general lassitude, extreme pain, loss of appetite, and vomiting. Shortly, the dog's fever will spike and severe diarrhea will set in. Dogs, especially puppies, suffer dehydration and weaken.

Symptoms: Symptoms of parvo's cardiac syndrome are most common in puppies. There is a loss of appetite, loud crying, and difficulty breathing. In this version of CPV, death may be sudden, but in some cases the animal lingers for days. Even when puppies survive the cardiac version of CPV, they may die months later from congestive heart failure.

Treatment: Treatment of CPV is difficult. It requires hospitalization, IV drips, and massive doses of antibiotics.

Prevention: As with distemper, the best treatment for CPV is prevention. Puppies should be kept away from public areas where infected dogs may have defecated. Inoculation is also important in preventing CPV. Most seven-in-one inoculations given by veterinarians include vaccines for parvo. Following the standard vaccination schedule for puppies, adult dogs should get annual boosters for CPV. In areas where parvo is a problem, semiannual boosters are recommended.

Through careful selection, good nutrition, and a regular schedule of inoculations, this beautiful puppy can grow to his potential.

Coronavirus

Coronavirus is a parvovirus-like disease. While seldom fatal, coronavirus can debilitate a dog to the point that it may die of other diseases. Symptoms of this disease include bloody diarrhea with a foul odor. Coronavirus is more easily prevented than cured. Vaccines are available for coronavirus alone or in combination with other vaccines. A single dose is given, followed by a second dose two to three weeks later. In situations where puppies must be vaccinated prior to 12 weeks of age, an additional dose should be administered between three and four months of age.

Parainfluenza

The common problem of kennel cough is frequently associated with the parainfluenza virus, although any number of other infections are known by the same name. The virus causes a

Young Border Collies like this one need to spend time at their veterinarian getting periodic checkups and vaccinations. These visits are also excellent opportunities to discuss such things as nutrition. At this age, a number of examinations for eye and vision problems should be administered.

condition known as tracheobronchitis. The classic symptoms of this infection are a constant hacking cough combined with a loud, abrasive retching. The parainfluenza virus may be spread by contact with infected animals or by living in an infected kennel. It can also be communicated through the water droplets coughed up by infected dogs and transported by the wind.

Fortunately, the infection caused by the parainfluenza virus is usually not a serious problem but run-down or sickly animals may become even more sickly if parainfluenza is not treated quickly. Likewise, otherwise healthy Border Collies may weaken if parainfluenza is allowed to linger.

Prevention: The parainfluenza vaccine is included in the combination inoculations given to puppies, so make sure your Border Collie has had the entire series of inoculations as a puppy.

Bordetella

Bordetella is a relatively mild bacterial infection that is frequently associated with tracheobronchitis. Its presence frequently complicates treatment of parainfluenza. It is easily controlled through vaccination so make sure your Border Collie is vaccinated against this opportunistic disease.

Tick–Borne Diseases

Borelliosis

Better known as Lyme disease, this is an infection that can prove fatal in both dogs and humans. It is transmitted through the bite of the common deer tick. It has also been reported that crushing an infected tick against the skin can result in infection. Borelliosis is found in all

50 states but is most common in coastal states. Infected dogs run a high fever, lose their appetite, and develop acute joint pain. A variety of other symptoms have also been attributed to Lyme disease, including enlarged lymph nodes and eye problems, as well as kidney and heart disease.

Diagnosing and treating Lyme disease is difficult. There is a simple blood test that tests for serum antibodies against Borelliosis, but unfortunately, the uninfected dogs can test positive at a much higher rate than most veterinarians would like. Also, if you find a deer tick attached to your dog, take the dog to the veterinarian after you have removed the tick. Be careful not to crush the tick between your fingers.

There is only one vaccination for Lyme disease available at the moment and it only has conditional approval. There is now a test for Lyme disease exposure in dogs, the Canine SNAP 3Dx . It can be performed in the office and has the benefit of discriminating between Lyme disease exposure and Lyme disease vaccine exposure. As with most canine diseases, the best cure for Lyme disease is to avoid it.

Treatment: By treating your Border Collie for ticks, using a good insect repellent, and avoiding known sites of infestation, you increase the chances of your dog not becoming infected with Lyme disease.

Rocky Mountain Spotted Fever

This is most commonly transmitted by the common dog tick in the East and the common wood tick in the West. Symptoms include fever, chills, abdominal pain, diarrhea, vomiting, bleeding of the mucous membranes, and some neurological symptoms. In extreme cases, RMSF can result in death.

Border Collies can serve a number of functions, but they can just be loved.

Treatment: RMSF is typically treated with tetracycline or doxycycline. If treatment begins quickly enough and the dog is sufficiently healthy, recovery should be rapid.

Ehrlichiosis

This is another disease carried by the brown dog tick. It is a potentially dangerous disease, for both dogs and humans.

There are three phases of symptoms for this disease:

Acute: Between two and four weeks after the tick bite, the dog will show enlarged lymph nodes, liver, and spleen. There will be lethargy, anemia, fever, depression, loss of appetite, joint pain, and stiffness. Subcutaneous bleeding will make lighter parts of the skin appear to be bruised.

Subclinical: Assuming that the afflicted dog has survived the acute phase, it will enter a quieter phase called the subclinical phase.

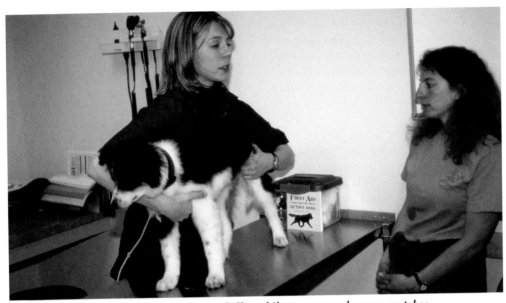

A veterinarian examines a young Border Collie while a concerned owner watches.

While the dog may not feel his best, he will do much better than during the acute phase. He may also pass off all the *ehrlichia*, the organism that causes the disease. If so, there will be a slow recovery. If not, the sick dog will enter the next phase.

Chronic: During this phase, there may be anemia, weight loss, neurological problems up to and including seizures, fever, and fluid accumulation in the hind legs.

It is common to see a drop in both red blood cells and white blood cells because ehrlichiosis attacks the bone marrow. Eventually, the bone marrow will begin to release immature white blood cells, which may cause some confusion between a diagnosis of ehrlichiosis and leukemia.

Treatment: Again, treatment is through the antibiotics tetracycline or doxycycline. For milder cases, treatment will run for two to three weeks. For more extreme cases, blood transfusions and/or intravenous fluids may be called for. Please understand that the outlook for dogs in the acute phase is pretty good. Dogs that have already entered the chronic phase do not have as good an outlook.

Babeosis

Babeosis is another disease carried most commonly by the brown dog tick. It may also be carried by deer ticks, dirty syringes, and through the mother dog's placenta. Young dogs will show loss of appetite, anemia, jaundice, fever, and loss of energy. Urine may be brown or red. Adult dogs will have lower fevers, anemia, and loss of appetite.

Treatment: There is currently only one treatment for babeosis, imidocarb diproprionate, and that product is only available from veterinarian.

Vaccinations

In recent years the practice of inoculating for "non-core" diseases has come into question in the minds of some veterinarians, even in some schools of veterinary medicine. The American Veterinary Medicine Association (AVMA) has recommended a different schedule for vaccinations for some "non-core" diseases such as bordetella, parainfluenza, and coronavirus (See *http://www.peteducation.com/ article.cfm?cls=2&cat=1648&articleid=950.*)

Note that no recommendations are absolute but depend on the condition of the dog, the age of the dog, the prevalence of the problem in the vicinity, and type of vaccine. In all cases, consult your veterinarian.

Another Border Collie puppy about to be surprised by veterinary practices.

Leptospirosis

Like most infectious canine diseases, leptospirosis is typified by fever, loss of appetite, depression, and listlessness. Dogs infected with leptospirosis frequently show a characteristic "hunchbacked" look due to kidney infection and pain. Sometimes ulcers will form on the mucous membrane of the mouth and throat. The dog may have extreme thirst, a thick brown coat on his tongue, and increased urination as a result of the kidney infection. Blood may also be present in the stool or from the mouth. It is not uncommon for the whites of the eyes to turn yellow.

Diarrhea and vomiting are other common symptoms. In spite of the unpleasant symptoms, "lepto" is usually relatively mild. Older dogs, sickly animals, or very young puppies suffer most from the disease.

Leptospirosis is one of those diseases covered by the so-called "eight-in-one" injections given as the puppy's first shots.

Other Health Problems

External Parasites

Fleas: Fleas are probably the most common external parasites found on dogs. Beyond the irritation and problems directly attributable to fleas, they are a common transport for other diseases and parasites. Tapeworms require the flea as a vector to get into the dog's system. Fleas cause itching, loss of hair, and, potentially, anemia. Most instances of canine eczema are related to flea infestations.

Fleas breed with amazing rapidity. Adult fleas lay eggs in whatever organic material is available. Damp bedding is a perfect place for incubating flea eggs. Six to twelve days after the eggs are laid, larval fleas hatch. The larvae eat organic material for a few days, and then spin a cocoon. When the adult female flea emerges from the cocoon, it immediately attaches itself

Border Collies make excellent rescue dogs, drug detection dogs, and companion dogs.

to the first dog, or other host, that comes along. After filling itself on blood, it begins laying eggs and the cycle starts all over. Since the female flea lays hundreds or thousands of eggs at a time, it is easy to see how these pests can overrun a kennel.

If a flea is found on a dog it is a sure bet that the dog's environment is infested. Simply treating the dog will give only temporary benefits. If there are fleas in the house, kennel, or yard, the dog will be reinfected when he is returned to the infested area.

The best treatment for fleas involves treating the dog, cleaning and treating his kennel, and treating other areas he frequents. The most effective treatment for fleas and tick are those chemicals applied to the back of the dog. The better products are good for a month and are highly effective.

Typically, these products are sold in packets of three tubes. The tubes have tips with crimps in them. By breaking the tips, the fluid is released. The fluid is then released on the skin by squeezing it along the backbone from the base of the tail to the collar. Talk to your veterinarian about the most effective of these products. You might also ask your veterinarian about an effective flea/tick collar to keep the pests off your Border Collie.

Ticks: These are typically found in dense brush and woods where there is a high mammal host population. As dogs brush up against bushes containing ticks, the tick attaches itself to the dog and quickly begins to suck blood. As discussed earlier, tick bites can cause skin irritation and spread potentially fatal diseases such as Lyme disease. Deer ticks are small (1 mm to 3 mm) and hard-shelled. They are the ticks that carry Lyme disease. The more common dog tick is larger and softer shelled.

The best way to prevent ticks is to keep your Border Collie away from infested areas, but this approach is not realistic for most owners. The best approach for controlling ticks on your Border Collie is a combination of living area treatment, regular treatment, and the application of insect repellents. Talk to your veterinarian about the most effective treatment regimen for your dog and the area.

Border Collies should be examined as often as possible for the presence of ticks. The dense undercoat of the breed makes it difficult to locate ticks. Smooth-haired Border Collies have the same undercoat and should receive the same close examination. Run your fingers through the hair on his back and sides, examine the area around and in the ears closely, checking the inside of the ears and the area just

Even when they're relaxing in the straw, Border Collies appear ready to spring into action.

above the eyes especially closely. Have the animal lie down so that you can check the stomach, the base of the tail, and lower portions of the chest.

✔ If you find ticks on your Border Collie, do not just pull them off. Simply pulling the tick off will very likely leave the parasite's head in your dog's skin, which almost always results in the area around the bite becoming infected.

✔ A better method of removing the parasites is to soak a cotton swab in alcohol and daub the area right on top of the bite. Next, using a pair of tweezers, grasp the tick as close to the skin as you can.

Caution: Never use unprotected fingers when trying to remove ticks as Lyme disease and other diseases can be transmitted to humans through contact with the skin.

✔ Pull the tick out of the dog's skin very slowly. Make sure that none of the tick is left attached to your dog.

✔ Apply more disinfectant to the area. Find something to do with the tick—flush it down the toilet, burn it, or crush it. Just make sure that it doesn't come in contact again with you or your Border Collie.

✔ If you find a large tick with one or more smaller ticks around it, you have found an adult female with male suitors. The little males have to be removed in the same manner as the larger females, and as carefully.

Ear Mites

Ear mites are another type of blood-sucking parasite that are obviously, from the name, found in the ears and ear canals. Dogs with ear mites will show excessive scratching of the ears and constant head shaking. Ear mites produce a dirty, waxy/greasy substance that adheres to the inside of the ear. While an ear mite infection is not life-threatening, it can cause your dog a great deal of discomfort and stress.

Examine your dog's ears frequently. If he shows any of the symptoms mentioned above, or has a waxy deposit in his ears, get him to a professional. Ear mites are transmitted through contact with other infected dogs. Regular examinations and professional care are especially important if you have more than one dog.

Mange

Mange is an inflammation of the skin caused by parasitic mites. The male mites remain on the surface while the females burrow up to an inch into the skin. After laying 20 to 40 eggs, the female dies. The newly hatched mites mature in about two weeks. During this time they live on blood and lymph. As a by-product of the mite's metabolism, it secretes a toxin that causes itching. Two types of mites produce two types of mange:

1. *Demodectic mange* is most common in younger dogs. This type of mange, often called red mange, is characterized by patchy hair loss.

2. *Sarcoptic mange* is sometimes called scabies. It causes the loss of large amounts of hair and intense itching and is particularly dangerous since it can pass from dog to human.

If your Border Collie shows symptoms of mange, take him to a veterinarian as quickly as possible. Beyond the obvious problems of discomfort and unsightly skin lesions, secondary infections can cause the infected dog to die.

Internal Parasites

One of the most important parts of a complete health management program for your Border Collie is the control of worms. Regular testing of feces and blood by the veterinarian can detect internal parasites before they become a major problem.

Treatment: This is best left to professionals. Veterinarians have access to a broader range of treatments than even experienced amateurs and are better versed in their use.

Dogs are most commonly affected by roundworms, hookworms, tapeworms, and heartworms. If you think your dog has internal parasites of any kind, get him to the veterinarian.

Heartworms: Forty or fifty years ago, heartworms were considered a problem only in Florida and the Gulf Coast area of the United States. Dogs in the Midwest, the Northeast, and desert areas of the United States almost never contracted heartworms; therefore, few veterinarians in those areas knew how to diagnose or treat the problem. Now, as a result of the increased mobility of the American public, heartworms are found in most parts of the country.

Heartworms are transmitted from infected dogs to uninfected dogs through a mosquito bite. In fact, the heartworm requires the mosquito as a host during part of its development.

✔ There are five stages, labeled L1 through L5, in the development of a heartworm. The young heartworms of the L1 stage are better known as *microfilaria*. It is in the L1 stage that *microfilaria* are sucked into the host mosquito when the dog is bitten.

✔ While in the mosquito, the *microfilaria* will progress through the L2 to the L3 stage.

✔ L3 stage heartworms move to the mosquito's mouth parts and wait until the mosquito bites a dog. The heartworm larvae are deposited on the dog's skin and crawl into the bite wound left by the mosquito.

✔ These larvae live in the dog's skin until they develop into L5 larvae, at which point they enter the infected animal's bloodstream, travel to the

Even though this puppy appears depressed, this method of flea and tick control is quick and easy.

pulmonary arteries, and develop into adult heartworms. There they start the cycle again.

Today, there is no real reason for dogs to develop clinical symptoms of heartworm infestations. Preventive treatment is available in daily and monthly dosages. Daily doses are easier to remember but forgetting a single day's dose can result in a heartworm infection. Monthly doses provide longer coverage, but may be harder to remember. Talk to your veterinarian about the best plan for your dog. Do not forget to fill him or her in on your work schedule, your social life, and your memory. Remember, though, that all such treatments do is kill *microfilaria*; adult heartworms are left alive but sterile.

If your Border Collie is unfortunate enough to develop clinical symptoms of a heartworm infestation, they will develop gradually. As the number of adult heartworms increases in the pulmonary arteries, blood flow is dramatically

reduced. Infected dogs will lose stamina, wheeze, cough, gag, and retch. They become listless and depressed. If the infestation is not treated, a slow death is certain. Blood flow in some dogs is reduced to the point that normally pink parts, such as the tongue, may turn blue.

Roundworms

If you notice that your Border Collie's coat has lost its shine, or that younger dogs have developed a massive belly, the dog may have roundworms. They are more common in puppies and young dogs. Roundworms are rarely fatal, but they reduce an animal's vitality and potential. Severe roundworm infestations, left untreated, may result in a stunted adult.

Dogs with roundworms will frequently vomit worms or pass them in their stools. At the first sign of roundworms, get your Border Collie to the veterinarian as soon as possible. Better yet,

Border Collies like this one can occur randomly in black and white litters. Avoid kennels that advertise Border Collies by color or pattern of color.

Hookworms are especially harmful to puppies, but can attack dogs of any age. Infected dogs may have bloody or tarry stools and become "unthrifty." They may lose their appetite, lose weight, or fail to gain weight. Some dogs may die due to anemia or complications from anemia.

Cleanliness: This is another case where clean kennels can reduce the chance of infestation. Combine cleanliness with regular checkups and treatment. An aggressive treatment program combined with rigorous kennel cleanliness should reduce the effects of hookworms.

Tapeworms

The tapeworm cycle begins with an infected host. Tapeworms deposit eggs in fecal matter. Some of this fecal matter clings to hair around the anus. Fleas inadvertently swallow the eggs. The tapeworm eggs undergo some development inside the flea and when the flea later bites the dog, the dog naturally chews at the bite. If it swallows an infected flea while it is gnawing, the dog is infected and an adult tapeworm will develop.

Stages: The first part of the tapeworm to develop is the head, or scolex. The scolex has several hooks around the top, which are used to attach the scolex to the lining of the stomach. Once attached, the tapeworm absorbs nutrients from the dog's stomach and shortly begins to produce body segments known as proglottids. The youngest, smallest proglottid is attached to the head; larger, more mature proglottids are at

prevent roundworm infestations in your Border Collie by keeping his kennel or living area clean.

Clean living areas: Dogs get roundworms through contact with roundworm-infected feces, but they may be infected in utero. By keeping your dog's living area stool-free, you decrease your dog's chances of infection. If they are born with roundworms, they can only be treated for them. Regular visits to the veterinarian for testing and treatment are also key to reducing damage by these parasites. Remember that dog food costs money, and every roundworm present in your dog takes some of what you are feeding the dog.

Hookworms

Hookworms get their name from the hooks they use to attach themselves to the host animal's stomach. Once attached, they go on to suck blood from the linings of the stomach and intestines.

the other end of the tapeworm. Tapeworms may have several thousand proglottids, each bigger and more mature than the one before it. Proglottids contain both ovaries and testes. By the time mature proglottids separate from the tapeworm, they will contain a number of fertilized eggs. Dog owners may notice what appears to be rice around the dog's anus. These "rice kernels" are the adult proglottids that have passed through the dog.

Note: Your Border Collie does not have to be heavily infested with fleas to contract tapeworms; it takes only one flea to convey the worms. Like roundworms they will absorb as much food as they can from your dog's stomach. If you see evidence of tapeworms on your dog, consult your veterinarian for treatment.

Emergencies

Poisons

Keeping a Border Collie away from poisons can be particularly difficult, as most of the poisons that he may encounter are not labeled. Even chocolate can kill a dog—a fatal dose can be surprisingly small.

There are many dangerous substances to watch out for in and around your home, such as:
• Most paint-related products such as paint removers, varnishes, turpentine, and oil-based paints.
• Kerosene, gasoline, diesel fuel, and cleaning fluid.
• Rat poisons, hand soaps, detergents, insecticides, mothballs, polishes, and some beauty products.
• Antifreeze. Unless prevented from doing so, dogs will drink antifreeze when they will not

drink water. It is widely held that antifreeze tastes sweet to dogs, although there is no way of determining exactly what the dogs find attractive about antifreeze.
• Various plants, including jimpson weed, mistletoe, foxglove, and poinsettia leaves, are as poisonous to dogs as they are to humans. Leaves of common ivy are also poisonous as are daffodils, tulip bulbs, lily of the valley, azaleas, wisteria, and delphiniums. Before you decorate or buy a potted plant, talk to your veterinarian or a good horticulturist concerning a plant's harmful potential.
• Contact with toads can cause your Border Collie to foam at the mouth and/or die.
• Some species of shrews are also poisonous.
• Spiders, scorpions, some flies, butterflies, and even cockroaches, may be fatally poisonous if eaten in enough quantity.

Treatment: If you have reason to believe that your dog has ingested a petroleum-based poison, an acid, or a strongly alkaline substance, *do not induce vomiting.* Call your veterinarian.
✔ If your dog can drink, give him as much milk as he will take.
✔ Have someone read the label on the container the poison came in to see if an antidote is identified. If the poison has an antidote and it is available, administer it.
✔ After you have exercised all these options, get your dog to the veterinarian as quickly as possible.

Purging: If the poison is of another type, induce vomiting by giving the dog a mixture of equal parts water and hydrogen peroxide. Try to give at least one tablespoon of the mixture per 10 pounds (4.5 kg) of body weight.
✔ Make a pocket of the dog's lips and pour a little of the mixture into the pocket at a time.

✔ Allow the dog time enough to swallow the liquid before giving him more.

✔ Vomiting should begin a few minutes after the final dose is administered. After vomiting ends, give the animal a teaspoon of Epsom Salts mixed with water to empty the intestines.

✔ When your pet is purged, take him to the veterinary emergency room as quickly as possible.

It is never a good idea to let your Border Collie on the couch or the bed. Not only does it leave hair all over, but the dog may also lose track of who is dominant in the relationship.

Heatstroke

Border Collies have been successfully worked in the most extreme environments; they work reindeer in Greenland and sheep in the deserts of Arizona. They are, however, susceptible to heatstroke. When you design and build your kennels, make sure that the dogs have sufficient shade in the warmer parts of the year. Also, be sure not to close up your dog in a car or truck at any time. Even in temperatures that may not seem warm to a human, the temperature in a vehicle can rise to dangerous levels. The bed of a pickup truck can also produce extremely high temperatures. If you make a habit of riding around in a truck with your Border Collie, remember that the practice is unsafe in a number of ways.

Another thing to remember about Border Collies is that they do not have an "off" switch.

This Border Collie suffered heatstroke and was packed in ice and rubbing alcohol in order to reduce excess body temperature.

If they become involved in something they enjoy doing, it is difficult to tell when they have become overheated. Quite a few ranchers and farmers have lost good dogs because they worked them up to the point where they died.

Keep a close watch on your dog. If he becomes dazed, runs a high fever, or shows extremely red gums and lips, get him to water. If you happen to be close to a garden hose, use it to soak the dog. If you are near a pond, pool, or water trough, put the dog in. If you are close enough to your emergency kit, soak the overheated Border Collie with alcohol and water, then get him to the veterinarian.

Administering Medicine

Liquids

When administering liquid medicine, pull the dog's lips into a pocket and pour the medicine into the lip pocket, holding the dog's mouth closed until he has swallowed all the medicine. Tilting the animal's head back too far or pouring the liquid medicine directly over the tongue can result in inhalation pneumonia, and pneumonia of any kind can result in death.

Pills

Pills are best administered by pressing your dog's lips firmly against his teeth, forcing his mouth open. Place the pill as far back on the dog's tongue as possible. Close the animal's mouth and hold it shut until you are certain that the pill has been swallowed. Stick around for a few minutes to make sure that the dog does not spit the pill out on the floor.

Using a large syringe, without a needle, is another, very effective method of administering liquid medication.

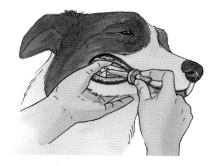

By cupping the lip, liquid medication may be administered to injured or sick Border Collies without drowning the dog or wasting medication.

HOW-TO: TREAT AUTOMOBILE

The Natural Enemy

Aside from poisons and diseases, the Border Collie's only natural enemy is the automobile. No matter how hard you may have tried to protect your dog from accidents, they may still happen. If an automobile strikes your dog, take the following steps:

1. Stay calm. Speak softly. Do not panic. If you go berserk, you can expect no more of your dog.

2. Loosen the dog's collar. Check his breathing passages for secretions or other blockages. If they exist, clear the passageways.

3. Protect yourself. Do not poke or prod at an injured dog. No matter how trustwor-thy your Border Collie has been in the past, all bets are off once he is injured. Many owners have been unpleasantly surprised when their pet mauled them as they were trying to relieve his discomfort. Before you try to examine your pet, make sure he is muzzled unless the injured dog is having difficulty breathing. If a commercially made muzzle is not available, make a temporary muzzle out of whatever you can find—leashes, belts, stockings, or neckties. Make a loop out of the object, cross the loose ends under the dog's muzzle and around his neck, and tie the ends securely behind the head. Test the muzzle to make sure the injured animal cannot bite.

4. Attend to any bleeding that you find. Clean the wound and apply pressure until the bleeding stops. Heavy bleeding may require that you apply more than one bandage. Keep applying bandages until the bleeding stops.

5. If the bleeding cannot be stopped with pressure, apply a tourniquet. Place the tourniquet between the heart and the wound and gradually increase the pressure until the bleeding stops. Once the bleeding has stopped, release the tourniquet every 15 minutes to keep the wound clean.

6. If there is a sucking chest wound involved, it must be plugged. The wound allows air to be drawn into the chest cavity rather than the lungs. Use a piece of plastic wrap or some other nonporous material to cover the wound, and some adhesive tape to secure the edges. The idea is to prevent air from entering the wound so that your dog will be able to breathe as normally as possible.

Stomach Wounds

Stomach wounds offer other problems. Cover exposed intestines with a wet, sterile dressing. It is important to keep the

A tourniquet is an effective method for stopping excessive bleeding when all other techniques have failed. It is potentially dangerous and should only be used when the application of pressure fails or when there is obvious arterial involvement.

ACCIDENT VICTIMS

intestines and organs from drying, to keep infection to a minimum, and to keep the intestines in the body cavity. Wrap the sterile dressing with a commercial bandage if it is available.

Do not attempt to push protruding intestines back into the stomach cavity. Pressure on the intestines may cause weak spots in the intestines to leak their contents into the body cavity, which can result in peritonitis, an infection of the lining of the stomach cavity. At best, peritonitis can be troublesome to the dog's recovery; at worst, it can be fatal.

Head Wounds

For head wounds, pressure should be applied using a gauze pad to reduce bleeding. Hold the pad in place with tape. Remember that even minor head wounds can bleed profusely. Make sure your pet is conscious and that he stays that way.

Puncture Wounds

Puncture wounds should be allowed to bleed for a few minutes, as the bleeding will help clean the wound. If bleeding is very heavy, apply pressure with a gauze pad. Hold the pad in place until the bleeding stops.

Shock Weakness and So On

Check for signs of shock weakness, pale gums, shivering, or a faint pulse. Keep the dog warm. Treat any bleeding wound he might have and try to keep him conscious.

Moving the Dog

Do not move the injured dog unless you must. Some veterinarians will come to accident sites, but if you must move your dog to go to the veterinarian, try to find help. Try to gently move the animal with a piece of plywood, a tarp, or even a large serving tray. If you have to

The best way to stop bleeding is through the use of pressure on the wound with a clean cloth or pad. In the case of true emergencies, the cleanliness of the pad or cloth is not as important as stopping the bleeding.

move the animal by yourself, try easing your pet onto a blanket. Then gently drag the injured animal to a vehicle and try to get him into it without causing further harm. Call ahead to make sure that someone will be waiting for you at the veterinary clinics. Hurry.

Under most circumstances, severely injured dogs should not be moved. In situations where it is better to move immediately, one method is to slide a large piece of strong material under the injured Border Collie and have adults lift it slowly and steadily to a vehicle.

Border Collie Registries

The American Border Collie Association Inc.
   (ABCA)
82 Rogers Road
Perkinston, MS 39573
(601) 928-7551
www.americanbordercollie.org

The American-International Border Collie
   Registry, Inc. (AIBC)
P.O. Box 274
Chapel Hill, TX 77426

The North American Sheep Dog Society (NASDS)
RR 3
McLeansboro, IL 62859

Canadian Border Collie Association (CBCA)
Box 424
Winchester, ON, K0C 2K0
www.canadianbordercollies.org

The International Sheep Dog Society (ISDS)
Clifton House
4a Goldington Road
Bedford, England MK40 3NF

All-Breed Registries

The American Kennel Club (AKC)
51 Madison Avenue
New York, NY 10010
(212) 696-8200
www.akc.org

For Registration Information:
The American Kennel Club (AKC)
5580 Centerview Drive
Suite 200
Raleigh, NC 27606

The United Kennel Club (UKC)
100 East Kilgore Road
Kalamazoo, MI 49001

The Kennel Club
I-4 Clarges Street, Piccadilly
London, W1Y8AB, England

Australian National Kennel Council
P.O. Box 1005
St. Marys, NSW 2760
Phone: +61 - 2 98 34 40 40
E-mail: dogsaust@ozemail.com.au
www.ankc.com

Border Collie Rescue

bcrnd.org/id27.htm

Border Collie Breed Clubs

The Border Collie Club of Great Britain
Firbeck, Worksop
Nottinghamshire, England

Border Collie Society of America, Inc (BCSA)
815 Royal Oaks Drive
Durham, NC 27712
(AKC Parent Club)

The United States Border Collie Club
Route 1, Box 83-D
Julian, PA 16844
(Non-AKC Breed Club)

Other Border Collie Clubs

The Border Collie Handlers Association
2915 Anderson Lane
Crawford, TX 76638
www.usbcha.com

Books

Allen, Arthur. *A Lifetime with the Working Collie, Their Training and History.* McLeansboro, IL: Self-published, 1979.

_____. *Border Collies in America.* McLeansboro, IL: Self-published, 1965.

Caius, D. J. *Of English Dogges.* London, 1570.

Carpenter, Barbara. *The Blue Riband of the Heather: The Supreme Champions 1906–88.* Ipswich: Farming Press, 1989.

Drabble, Phil. *One Man and His Dog.* London: Michael Joseph, 1984.

Fogt, Bruce. *Lessons from a Stock Dog: A Training Guide.* Sidney, Ohio: The Working Border Collie, Inc. (1996)

Grew, Sheila. *Key Dogs from the Border Collie Family.* Hernando, MS: Heritage Farms, 1993.

Halsall, Eric. *British Sheepdogs.* London: International Sheepdog Society, 1992.

_____. *Sheepdogs, My Faithful Friends.* London: P. Stephens, 1980.

Jones, H. Glyn and Barbara Collins. *A Way of Life: Sheepdog Training, Handling and Trialling.* Ipswill: Farming Press, 1987.

McCaig, Donald. *Nop's Trials.* New York: Crown, 1984.

_____. *Eminent Dogs, Dangerous Men.* New York: Harper/Collins, 1991.

Mundell, Matt. *Country Diary.* Edinburgh: Gordon Wright Publishing, 1981.

Robertson, Pope. *Anybody Can Do It.* Elgin, TX: Rovar Publ., 1979.

Scrimgeour, Derek. *Talking Sheepdogs.* Preston, UK: Farming Books and Videos, 2002.

Simpson, Julie. *The Natural Way.* York, UK YO42 1SU, *Working Sheepdog News*, 2003.

Border Collie puppies fluctuate from high energy/high speed to immediate sleep.

Periodicals

American Border Collie
P.O. Box 58
Patrick Springs, VA 24133

Borderlines
322 Spring Branch Lane
Kennedale, TX 76060
Fax: (817) 561-2662

The Working Border Collie Magazine
14933 Kirkwood Road
Sidney, OH 45365

United States Border Collie Club Newsletter
1712 Hertford Street
Greensboro, NC 27403

Working Sheepdog News
5 Vale Crescent, Bishop Wilton
York, England YO42 1SU
E-mail: *workingsheepdog@hotmail.com*

INDEX

About the Author

Mike DeVine has owned and trained Border Collies for many years. He has an M.A. in Psychology with an emphasis on cortical functioning and learning. He has edited and published *The Southern Stockdog Journal*, an internationally distributed magazine for those interested in working Border Collies. He is a life member of the North American Sheepdog Society (NASDS) and the American Border Collie Association (ABCA).

Important Note

This pet owner's guide tells the reader how to buy and care for a Border Collie. The authors and the publisher consider it important to point out that the guidelines presented in this book apply primarily to normally developed dogs from a reputable breeder—that is, to dogs in good health and of good character.

Anyone who adopts an adult dog should be aware that its personality might already have been influenced by other people. If possible, meet the previous owner and assess the interaction between the owner and the dog. If there is an affectionate relationship between them, you can be assured that, given some adjustment time, the dog will bond to you in the same way. If the dog comes from an animal shelter or rescue organization, the personnel in those organizations are trained to assess the personalities of dogs that come to them. Dogs with severe behavioral problems that cannot adapt to a new environment are not offered for adoption by either animal shelters or rescue organizations. Rescue organizations place dogs in homes with experienced owners, where they are evaluated, trained as necessary, and kept until they are placed as pets in permanent homes.

Animal shelters and rescue organizations see to it that the dog has all the necessary immunizations. If you are acquiring an adult dog from a private party be sure to get all of the health records from the previous owner. In any case, you will want to make arrangements to have your pet seen by your veterinarian before long.

Even well-behaved and carefully supervised dogs sometimes do damage to someone else's property or cause accidents. It is therefore in the owner's interest to be adequately insured against such eventualities, and we strongly urge all dog owners to purchase a liability policy that covers their dog(s).

Photo Credits

Norvia Behling: 9, 14, 15, 17, 25, 27, 31, 33, 42, 44, 58, 74, 78, 79, 82, 85, 88, and 93; Kent Dannen: 8, 13, 26, 48, 51, 53, 55, 56 (top and bottom), and 57; Tara Darling: 6, 18, 20, 21, 30, 43, 50, 70, 73, 80, and 83; Cheryl Ertelt: 5, 16, 32, 36, 37, 38, 46, 61, 63, 64, 65, and 76; Isabelle Francais: 2–3, 4, 7, 10, 11, 23, 24, 28, 29, 34, 39, 41, 54, 67, 71, 77, 81, 86, and 89; Pets by Paulette: 49 and 59; and Connie Summers: 40.

Cover Photos

Front cover: Karen Hudson; Inside Front Cover: Cheryl Ertelt; Inside Back Cover: Tara Darling; Back Cover: Isabelle Francais.

All inquiries should be addressed to:
Barron's Educational Series, Inc.
250 Wireless Boulevard
Hauppauge, NY 11788
www.barronseduc.com

ISBN-13: 978-0-7641-3644-3
ISBN-10: 0-7641-3644-5

Library of Congress Catalog Card No. 2006032080

Library of Congress Cataloging-in-Publication Data
DeVine, Michael, 1946–
    Border collies : everything about purchase, care, nutrition, behavior, and training / Michael DeVine; illustrations by Michele Earle-Bridges.
        p. cm. — (A complete pet owner's manual)
    Includes index.
    ISBN-13: 978-0-7641-3644-3
    ISBN-10: 0-7641-3644-5
    1. Border collie. I. Title.

SF429.B64D49   2007
636.737'5—dc22   2006032080

Printed in China
9 8 7 6 5 4 3 2 1